Classical World series

ARISTOPHANES AND HIS THEATRE OF THE ABSURD

Paul Cartledge

Bristol Classical Press

General Editor: John H. Betts

First published in 1990 by

Bristol Classical Press

an imprint of

Gerald Duckworth & Co. Ltd

48 Hoxton Square, London N1 6PB

Reprinted 1992

A catalogue record for this book ia available from the British Library

ISBN 1-85399-114-7

Printed in Great Britain by
The Cromwell Press, Melksham, Wiltshire

FOR GEOFFREY DE STE. CROIX

Contents

Illustrations

Preface

Scope

The Joint Association of Classical Teachers (JACT) sponsors a Classical Civilisation 'A' Level paper entitled 'Aristophanes and Athens'. Five plays are prescribed reading (currently *Acharnians*, *Clouds*, *Frogs*, *Lysistrata*, *Wasps*), from three of which passages are set for comment (*Acharnians*, *Clouds* and *Frogs* in 1990). The syllabus enjoins that Aristophanes be studied first as 'a major comic playwright' and secondly as 'the focus for an examination of Athenian society in the years during which his plays were first performed' (427-c. 385 BC: see A Brief 'Life' of the Poet, below). These two aims are in fact inseparable, since all Old Comedy, not just Aristophanes' plays, was quintessentially the product of 'Athenian society' and is unthinkable in isolation from it. But in this little book, which is of course not only written for those doing JACT papers, I shall be focussing more on Aristophanes than on Athens. I shall, though, endeavour to provide enough material on the latter, not least the religious aspect of Athenian society (esp. ch. 1), to make the plays' indispensable context intelligible.

The sorts of questions that I shall be posing – and sometimes tentatively suggesting answers to – are these: is it correct and feasible to look for any serious 'line' or 'message' underlying comic drama? If so, is the standpoint of Old Comedy in general and Aristophanes in particular anti-democratic or just sceptical towards all forms of authority, divine as well as human? Does Aristophanes' typical 'comic hero' (or 'anti-hero') represent or correspond to the 'ordinary Athenian' of the decades on either side of 400 BC? Does Aristophanic fantasy necessarily carry any practical implications?

I stress my use of 'tentatively' (above). In our desire to understand better this most remarkable ancient society at a climactic point in its history, there is a huge temptation to recycle as much as we can of the unique corpus of contemporary evidence provided by Aristophanes. That temptation must be resisted – or at any rate restrained. For reasons that will become clear later, we know much less about Aristophanic comedy than we would like to or need to know before we can use it confidently to recreate and interpret Athenian social, political, economic or intellectual conditions. We cannot simply assume, as one otherwise distinguished scholar once did, that it 'pictures reality, the real pulsating body of life'; Aristophanes should never be taken at face value as a source of evidence. Nor, unfortunately, is it possible to *demonstrate* (as opposed to making a plausibly strong case for) any general or particular interpretation of, say, Aristophanes' political outlook as a whole or 'the message' of the *Lysistrata* in particular.

On the other hand, there is no cause to apologise for yet another attempt to 'read' Aristophanes. As my Postscript attempts to make plain, Aristophanes has from one point of view – freedom of thought and expression – no less contemporary relevance for our society than he had for his own 2400 years ago (AD 1990 is in fact precisely the 2400th anniversary of the first performances of *Lysistrata* and *Thesmophoriazusae*). More mundanely, his plays are still put on today both in the original (as here at Cambridge, most recently the *Lysistrata* in 1986) and in a variety of modern vernacular translations. Moreover, they are still found funny, even if the sources and forms of the humour differ from modern production to modern production almost as much as they differ from the original sources and forms on show in the plays' first (and usually only) performance in the Theatre of Dionysos at Athens.

Arrangement

Rather than dealing with the plays in chronological sequence I have preferred to organise the discussion by topic, concentrating on one or more plays to illustrate each. This does not of course mean that a particular play can and should be read solely or even mainly in the light of one particular theme or topic. To take the most obvious instance, the theatricality of Aristophanes is not on exhibition solely or mainly in the *Thesmophoriazusae*, but equally in each and every one of the eleven more or less completely surviving plays.

Dedication and acknowledgements

Almost sixty years ago Gilbert Murray, Regius Professor of Greek at Oxford and tireless advocate of peace between the nations, dedicated his still usable study of Aristophanes to George Bernard Shaw –

'Lover of Ideas and Hater of Cruelty who has filled many lands with laughter and whose courage has never failed'. Whether or not we agree with Murray that Aristophanes was a sort of proto-Shaw, it is to the same kind of public – and one member of it in particular – that I dedicate this *biblion* (cf. *Birds* 574).

It remains only to thank Michael Gunningham, a tireless worker for JACT among his many other services to the Classics, and Kim Richardson and Eleanor Porter of BCP for commissioning and publishing this little book; Pat Easterling for steering me unexpectedly in an Aristophanic direction; Edith Hall and Simon Goldhill for their sadly unavailing attempts to sharpen my lit-critical wits and remedy my fathomless ignorance; and by no means least, Mr Catchpole and Ms Alison Mable of Heffer's bookshop in Cambridge for their user-friendly bibliopoly over many years.

Fig. 1. Map of Attica.

A Brief 'Life' of the Poet

The genre of biography was barely conceived, not yet even in its infancy, during the lifetime of Aristophanes. So the ancient *Life* of Aristophanes that survives from the post-Classical, Hellenistic age of scholarship (roughly the last three centuries BC) not only is very brief but consists largely of a mere stringing together of passages from his plays which the ancient scholiasts (commentators) considered to be reliably autobiographical. Our principal objective sources, therefore, are the official State records of the plays put on at the two 'national' (as opposed to local) dramatic festivals, the Lenaia and (Great or City) Dionysia. These may sometimes be supplemented by the *Hypotheses* (introductory remarks on place and date of performance, etc.) compiled by the far from infallible Hellenistic scholars.

The following table is intended to mark the major political and dramatic events relevant to comprehending the career of Aristophanes (though it should be added that 'dramatic' events were in themselves also 'political' events, since theatre at Athens was always an affair of the *polis* or 'state': see chapter 1). Dates in the form '487/6' indicate the duration of a civil year, which the Athenians named after their senior annual civilian official, the Chief or Eponymous Archon: in this instance, roughly July 487 to July 486. All plays were performed in the second half of an archon-year: thus the *Banqueters* of (in our terms) early 427 belongs strictly to 428/7.

Chronological table

(Many dates are approximate. All are BC.)

600	Dramatic choruses (esp. dithyrambs, choral lyrics sung to Dionysos) at Corinth and Sikyon
535	Tragic drama introduced into Dionysia, performed somewhere in Agora; Thespis credited with invention of solo speaker (hence actors today are 'Thespians')
508/7	Foundation of democracy

500	Primitive 'theatre' created in precinct of Dionysos
490	First Persian invasion: Battle of Marathon
✕ 487/6	Comic drama incorporated in Dionysia
480-79	Second Persian invasion: Battles of Thermopylae, Salamis, Plataia
449	Contest of tragic actors introduced
446/5	Thirty Years' Peace between Athens and Sparta: Athens recognises Sparta's Peloponnesian League, Sparta recognises Athenian Empire
445/4	**Birth of Aristophanes**
442	Contest of comic actors introduced
440	Tragedy and comedy introduced at Lenaia
440/39-437/6	Some legal restriction placed on comic abuse
431-404	Peloponnesian War between Athens and Sparta
427	*Banqueters* (Lenaia, 2nd prize). Produced by Kallistratos
426	*Babylonians* (Dionysia, ?1st prize). Produced by Kallistratos
425	Acharnians (Lenaia, 1st prize). Produced by Kallistratos
424	*Knights* (Lenaia, 1st prize)
423	*Clouds* (Dionysia, 3rd prize) [Surviving text is of the revised version of c. 418/7]
422	*Wasps* (Lenaia, 2nd prize). Produced by Philonides
421	*Peace* (Dionysia, 2nd prize). Peace of Nikias concluded, followed by Athens-Sparta alliance
415-13	Sicilian expedition; scandals of Herms- and Mysteries-desecration
414	*Birds* (Dionysia, 2nd prize)
411	*Lysistrata* (?Lenaia, ?prize). Produced by Kallistratos. *Thesmophoriazusae* (?Dionysia, ?prize). Produced by Kallistratos
411-10	Counter-revolution of the 400, Government of the 5000, restoration of democracy
406	Deaths of Sophocles and Euripides
405	*Frogs* (Lenaia, 1st prize). Produced by Philonides Euripides' *Bacchae* (Dionysia)
?404 (or ?403)	Repeat performance of *Frogs* (?Dionysia)
404	Athenian surrender (March/April), followed by

	Sparta's imposition of 30 Tyrants (summer)
403	Democracy restored, general amnesty
399	Trial and execution of Socrates
?392	*Ecclesiazusae* (?festival, ?prize)
388	*Plutus* (?festival, ?prize)
385	**Death of Aristophanes**

Aristophanes' official name in full was *Aristophanēs Philippou Kudathenaieus* or 'Aristophanes son of Philippos of [the *dēmos* = 'deme', i.e. village, parish, ward] Kydathenaion'. Kydathenaion was both an urban deme – it lay within the city-walls of Athens, rebuilt after the Persian sack of 480-79 – and a very large deme, in fact the third largest in terms of citizen manpower of all the 100 or more demes recognised when the democracy was founded in 508/7. Aristophanes' great-grandfather will have been living there when Kleisthenes' reforms required all the freeborn adult (eighteen-plus) male residents of Attica to have their names placed on their local deme-register in order to qualify as citizens of the new democracy.

Aristophanes was born in about 445, when Athens and Sparta swore the first of their shortlived peaces. His mother was, we may be sure, an Athenian woman, since Pericles' law of 451 had laid down that only the legitimate male offspring of an Athenian father *and* an Athenian mother could become Athenian citizens. But her name is, as usual, unknown: 'respectable' Athenian women were not supposed to be spoken of in the public, masculine sphere. The name of Aristophanes' father, on the other hand, is on record since, as we have seen, it formed part of the playwright's own official name. And a sociologically revealing name it is too: Philippos, 'he who loves horses', was appropriate only in a family rich enough to breed or at any rate own horses, and that means a very rich family indeed.

Some horse-breeding or horse-owning Athenians indulged in horse-racing, either at the local Panathenaic Games or at one of the Panhellenic festivals (of which the Olympic Games was the 'blue-riband' competition). But most contented themselves with serving in the small and militarily ineffective but socially privileged Athenian cavalry. The relevance of this to the *Knights* of 424 (when Aristophanes would have been just old enough for military service) and to the Socrates-corrupted son called Pheidi*pp*ides in the *Clouds* of 423 should be apparent. But it may be worth stressing that Aristophanes, whose own name meant 'eminently best', belonged to the Athenian aristocracy of birth and wealth.

There is some reason (an inference from *Acharnians* 652-4) for thinking that Aristophanes' father acquired a residence on Aigina after that island ('the eyesore of the Peiraeus' in Pericles' vivid metaphor) had been forcibly colonised by Athens at the outbreak of the Peloponnesian War. This would certainly have provided him and his family with a useful retreat from the Great Plague which afflicted the city of Athens between 430 and 426 especially. But there is equally good reason for supposing that Aristophanes somehow maintained or re-established an urban base in Kydathenaion, not least the fact that a certain Kleon was one of his fellow-demesmen. There is something peculiarly urban about Aristophanes (the Greek word *asteios* meant both 'urban' and 'urbanely witty'), and the 'face-to-face' quality of inner-city deme life would have intensified the friction between him and Kleon, his (real or stage-managed) *bête noire*.

'First novels' are very often more or less thinly disguised autobiography, and that rule-of-thumb can probably also be applied to Aristophanes' debut play *Banqueters*, performed at the Lenaia of 427 when he was perhaps seventeen or eighteen. At any rate, given its educational theme anticipating that of *Clouds* (see the back-reference at *Clouds* 528ff.), Aristophanes had very likely been treated to the novel, 'sophistic' instruction in rhetorical argumentation that was being eagerly consumed by members of his leisure-class social stratum in cosmopolitan, imperial, democratic Athens (see chapter 3).

Banqueters, however, like his next two productions, appeared not under his own name but under that of his producer Kallistratos. Whatever the reason for this inaugural pseudonymity (not confined to his prentice pieces), it did not, it seems, deceive Kleon. For if we can believe the choral *parabasis* (see chapter 2) of *Acharnians*, Kleon had gone to the lengths of lodging an official complaint against Aristophanes for abusing the Athenians in his *Babylonians* of 426. However, if Aristophanes was born in 444, perhaps what Kleon had really done was object to his father's registering him as a fellow-demesman and so Athenian citizen, possibly on the grounds of his Aiginetan connection. That sort of mudslinging was a normal feature of intra-deme political infighting between political enemies. And to translate that rather sordid private quarrel into 'national' theatrical terms would have been a characteristic piece of Aristophanic humour and self-promotion.

In any event, in 424 Aristophanes shed the mask of pseudonymity and presented his viciously anti-Kleon *Knights* in his own person, thereby winning his second (or possibly third) first prize (see chapter 5). In all, between 427 and his death in c. 385 he had performed some forty plays and won at least half a dozen first prizes. Of these just eleven survive, three of which are known to have been **winners**, all at the Lenaia.

Fig. 2. Marble head of Aristophanes (?), Roman period. (Uffizi Museum, Florence.)

Their author too was a survivor. He lived through the Great Plague, two bloodstained bouts of anti-democratic counter-revolution, and defeat in an unusually prolonged war followed by famine and enemy occupation, not to mention the hardships and losses that warfare routinely entailed. It was no accident that he wrote two plays entitled *Plutus* ('Wealth'), the second produced in 388 towards the end of yet another ten-year conflict (see chapter 7). His last two plays were produced under the byline of his second son, Araros. A new name, a new generation, a new dramatic and political era had come to be, as Aristophanes with his usual acumen and foresight had realised.

Chapter 1

High Days and Holidays: the Dionysiac Experience

'Nothing to do with Dionysos'

The *Frogs* is generally reckoned today to be the finest of Aristophanes' eleven surviving plays. Not only was he awarded a civic crown of sacred olive after its original victorious showing at the Lenaia of 405, but the play was also staged again during his own lifetime, indeed probably within a year of its first performance. In the fourth century some tragedies of Aeschylus were given a second airing, long after the playwright's death in 456, at a time when the Athenian tragic muse was in steep decline. But comedy after Aristophanes experienced no such deterioration, and it was Aristophanes whose posthumous decline was precipitous (see further, Postscript). What was it then that justified the precipitate revival of *Frogs*?

Our Hellenistic commentator was sure he knew: it was the famous *parabasis* (see chapter 2 for meaning of this), in which the Chorus dressed as raggedly-clothed initiates of the Eleusinian Mysteries made their plea ostensibly in the playwright's name for tolerance towards those Athenians who had 'mistakenly' been rather too energetic in the oligarchic cause during the troubled events of 411 (see chapter 5). That commentator was neither the first nor the last to treat an Aristophanic *parabasis* as a piece of deadly serious and 'straight' political rhetoric; and that reading of the *parabasis* would certainly help to explain the play's restaging in either 404 or 403, when reconciliation and tolerance towards oligarchs were unusually topical political themes. A more mundane reason for the repeat, though, might simply have been the difficulty of writing, commissioning and producing new plays during the upheavals of 405-3. But whatever the real reasons, I am sure that it was not for the *parabasis* alone, or even mainly, that *Frogs* was awarded first prize at its original performance. The principal reason, I venture to guess, was the role Aristophanes wrote for Dionysos.

1

Fig. 3. Attic red-figure cup attributed to Makron, c. 490 BC (Villa Giulia Museum, Rome). Dionysos dances ecstatically, drinking-horn in right-hand, thyrsus in left.

An ancient adage, more applicable to tragedy than to comedy, held that drama was 'nothing to do with Dionysos'. This was just a particularly vivid way of saying that there seemed to be nothing about the cult of Dionysos which necessarily and uniquely tied it to dramatic representations. Indeed, modern scholars share the perplexity of the ancients, and there is no agreed view on either the origins of Attic drama as such or on how and why drama should have been associated in Athens and Attica exclusively with various forms of the cult of Dionysos. Comedy, however, was more obviously connected with this god than was tragedy, even though it acquired dramatic form and official recognition later than tragedy. For the *kōmos* was a typically rustic rout or revel celebrating some high day or holiday within the annual agricultural cycle and was liberally lubricated by the *spécialité* of Dionysos' *maison*, the fermented juice of the wine-grape. Still, there was no inevitable reason why the songs (*ōidai*) that accompanied the *kōmos* – hence *kōmōidia* – should have become formalised into comic drama.

On the other hand, once the connection had for whatever reason been made, it was a relatively straightforward one for the comic (as opposed to the tragic) poet to exploit. 'Wine, women and song' is a time-honoured masculine formula, and although real Athenian women played major parts in various cults of Dionysos (most famously or notoriously the sort of maenadic cult explored so savagely in Euripides' *Bacchae* just a couple of months after the first performance of *Frogs*), by a dramatic convention all the performers at the Dionysia and later the Lenaia festivals (dithyrambic choristers, chorus-members, actors, and probably the non-speaking extras too) were of the male sex.

Hence sexuality thrust itself forward as a naturally dominant Dionysiac theme, aided by Dionysos' ritual implication with fertility and growth. The wearing of the erect phallos by at least some of the actors in comic drama corresponded to the exaggeratedly male-dominated quality of the sexuality celebrated in Dionysiac rituals both on (as in the personified Phales of *Acharnians* 263-79) and off the stage. From sexuality and fertility it was a short step to bawdiness and obscenity of language and gesture, in Dionysiac drama as in real-life Athenian religious cults – for example, in the annual celebration of the Eleusinian Mysteries, which was open to both sexes, or the married women-only Thesmophoria. Finally, the wearing of masks (*prosōpa*, Latin *personae*) by all the performers in comedy may have had its origin in pre-dramatic mumming, but it was also well adapted to the peculiarly Dionysiac experiences of *ekstasis* (standing outside oneself) and *enthousiasmos* (receiving the god within oneself). Both involved a change of personality (as we say, in unconscious homage to the Latin etymology); and the easiest way to create the illusion of becoming someone else is to assume a mask.

In short, comedy at least did have rather a lot to do with Dionysos inasmuch as that god of fertility, regeneration and wine was a potent catalyst of self-liberating personality change. But that change occurred, and was allowed to occur, only within a controlled environment, that of state-sponsored religious rituals allotted their appropriate time and space within the civic festival calendar and communal civic space (see below).

Aristophanes' Dionysos: 'rather ungodlike'?

In comedy, as in all carnival, there is an ingrained tendency for the norms of 'ordinary' life to be suspended, subverted or even turned on their heads. Aristophanes' Dionysos in *Frogs* exploits this tendency to the utmost. For 'he' turns out to be remarkably feminine, kitted out in a yellow dress and with a yellow (i.e. cowardly) streak in his nature to match. He, a god, changes places with his slave – a typically saturnalian motif aping the annual reversal of these roles at harvest-time by real men and their slaves, but given here by Aristophanes a 'naturalistic' twist, since his cowardly and effeminate Dionysos seems naturally servile. Dionysos' borrowing of the dress and equipment of the utterly virile Herakles serves merely to highlight his inadequacies above ground, which are exposed in a darker hue during his journey to Hades. The low point, perhaps, is reached when he shits himself in terror at the subterranean horrors of Tartaros (*Frogs* 479). But he scarcely acquits himself better when, as the divine patron of drama, he is called upon to exercise his (non-existent) artistic sensibilities in the life-and-death contest (*agōn*) to find the best of the dead tragic poets – 'best' in the sense of the one most able to save the city of Athens in its time of military, political and especially spiritual crisis.

There is more at stake in our interpretation of Aristophanes' Dionysos than mere judgment of his creation's artistic quality and merit. It would scarcely be an exaggeration to say that here lies one of the keys to unlocking the mystery of classical Athenian religion. For this Aristophanic Dionysos has been called 'rather ungodlike', which raises the question of just exactly what the Athenians did consider their gods to be like. Since they depicted them in their words and images in human form, anthropomorphically, it is tempting to agree with one leading authority that they were 'larger Greeks', superhuman beings, beyond the human partly because of their irresistible powers, partly thanks to their immortality.

To this view, however, two objections apparently arise. First, how does one square the remarkably, indeed pathetically human Dionysos of Aristophanes with, say, the Euripidean earthquake-delivering, mania-inducing Dionysos, let alone with the life-enhancing, consciousness-raising, mind-blowing Dionysos worshipped by the many Greeks of both sexes who chose to be initiated into Dionysiac mystery-cults that had nothing to do with the theatre?

Does one simply dismiss the Aristophanic god as a buffoon, a joke, a feaster in a banquet of licensed blasphemy? Or does one rather regard him as a figure of wish-fulfilment, deliberately made ridiculous for a finite and short time in a play, precisely because, when the Greeks were not playing, Dionysos was not at all a matter for ribald laughter but a force to be reckoned with?

This latter possibility leads into the other objection to the 'larger Greeks' view. Are the Olympian gods best seen as 'persons' at all, or should they not rather be assimilated to the other, usually collectively anonymous but always supernaturally and superhumanly powerful, divine agencies by which the Greeks felt their world to be moulded and manipulated – the Fates, the Furies, the Avenging Ones, and so on? In that case, calling the Aristophanic Dionysos 'rather ungodlike' would be an understatement, since he has clearly trespassed too far on the human side of the human/divine divide to qualify any longer for godhead.

The prudent answer to this conundrum, then, is perhaps to say that, in a manner desperately alien to post-mediaeval Christian ideas, the Greek and Athenian conception of deity embraced a little of all these seemingly contradictory versions of Dionysos. The same people whose 'official' explanation of why the gods got only the smell and not the substance of an animal sacrifice was that the Titan Prometheus had once tricked almighty Zeus, and who believed that the gods were obligated to repay the favour even of a mere sacrificial smell, could also see themselves in Shakespearian terms 'as flies to wanton boys', to be killed – like Pentheus in the *Bacchae* – for the gods' sport.

The Aristophanic Dionysos, then, was meant to be funny, but that was only part of this god's 'story' (*mythos*). Nor do I think it mere chance that for his main Chorus in *Frogs* Aristophanes chose a company of initiates in the Eleusinian Mysteries. Less than two years before, Alcibiades, who had been convicted of sacrilege for profaning the Mysteries in 415, had made a point of leading the Eleusinian procession after his pardon and return to Athens in 407; now in exile once again, Alcibiades was the major political talking-point of early 405. But apart from its topicality, the choice of Eleusinian initiates would also reassure the audience that the religious proprieties were not being entirely neglected even in the topsy-turvy carnivalesque world of the *Frogs*. Through their unremitting observance of this native but panhellenic cult (the Mysteries themselves were never good for a joke) they, the Athenians of the *theatron*, were justifying their status among the gods' elect and helping to preserve the balance of nature.

Festivals of democracy: the Lenaia and Dionysia

Theatron originally was the collective noun for a group of *theatai* (spectators) and so became used for the place where the spectators spectated. In the Athens of Aristophanes that meant the Theatre of Dionysos cut into the south-east slope of the Acropolis hill. The technicalities of staging, including the physical setting of the dramas, will be dealt with in the following chapter. Here we shall be concerned with the religio-political, festival context within which the plays were just one, and not necessarily the most important, element.

Festivals were the beating heart of classical Greek religion. Above 300 such public, state-organised festivals are on record as being celebrated at more than 250 locales throughout the Greek world in honour of over 400 different deities (if we count Dionysos Lenaios as separate from Dionysos Eleuthereus, for example, as we properly should). The Athenians were particularly 'into' festivals, proud that they devoted up to 144 days of their calendar to them, more than any other Greek *polis*. The high number is explained chiefly by the size, diversity and historical origins of the Athenian state. By the time of Aristophanes' birth Attica, the 2400 square kilometres that constituted the state's territory (about the size of Luxembourg – or Derbyshire), had long been united and centrally administered. But in the years immediately surrounding his birthdate a second, no less important, political development had been the extension of democratic notions into the field of the state religion. Thus the Lenaia and more especially the Great or City Dionysia were not just religious festivals, but specifically democratic religious festivals, reflecting the Athenians' remarkable and pioneering development of this novel form of self-government. It was of the essence of democratic thinking that not just the social elite but all Athenian citizens should be able to participate equally in these relaxing and renovating holy-days.

The junior of the two dramatic festivals was the Lenaia, which is also far less well documented than the Great Dionysia. It was included in the festival calendar of sacrifices, inscribed on stone within the *Stoa Basileios* (see below) in the Athenian agora. There it duly appeared under the wedding month of Gamelion, sandwiched between two other festivals of Dionysos – the Rural Dionysia in Poseideion (which Dikaiopolis, hero of *Acharnians*, was so desperately longing to

celebrate in peace: see chapter 6) and the Anthesteria in Anthes-
terion. The latter was a spring festival, and particularly a wine-festival
(see *Acharnians* 1000-2), of great antiquity. Thus between December
and March in our terms there was a Dionysiac mini-cycle within the
greater Athenian festival cycle as a whole, placed there no doubt to
compensate for the terrifying hiatus in visible plant-growth that was
the hallmark of a Mediterranean winter.

The *Stoa Basileios* or 'Royal Portico' was the official residence
of the Basileus or 'King'. But this king was no absolute monarch;
rather he was an annually selected civic official chosen since 487/6 by
the democratic procedure of the lot and since 457/6 from a potential
pool of candidates that included the majority of Athenian citizens.
Nor was he even a priest: it was a distinguishing mark of all ancient
Greek culture that no priesthood in any state had ever acquired the
authority to define orthodoxy or utter dogmas, and it was utterly
typical that the titular head of Athenian religion should not have been
a religious specialist. All the same, his was an onerous and honorific
post, with responsibility for overseeing most aspects of the state
religion. He it was who supervised the administration of the Lenaia,
including, from about 440 on, the staging of both tragedies and
comedies. And it was at the Lenaia, an intimately Athenian festival
by contrast to the more international Dionysia (see *Acharnians*
502-8), that *Frogs* was first put on.

However, it was not only by plays (performed almost certainly
in the Theatre of Dionysos, like those of the later Dionysia) that
Dionysos Lenaios (Dionysos of the wine-vat?) was worshipped on the
twelfth to (roughly) fifteenth days of Gamelion. In fact, the central
religious phenomenon of the Lenaia, as of the Dionysia, was the ritual
procession to Dionysos' sanctuary followed by animal sacrifice and a
rare meat supper.

A politically administered theatre

Still, the plays – or rather their impresarios and authors – were
politically important enough for a Basileus to think it worthwhile
publicly to commemorate them. On the surviving base of a herm,
which 'Onesippos son of Aitios of Kephisia dedicated' in about 400,
he saw fit to mention that during his term of office Sosikrates and
Stratonikos were the winning *khorēgoi* or impresarios and Nikokhares
and Megakleides the winning playwrights for comedy and tragedy
respectively.

Onesippos, it goes without saying, had not been chosen as Basileus for his dramatic knowledgeability and appreciation of theatre. No more of an expert was his senior colleague in the Archonship, the Archon (or Eponymous Archon), to whose lot fell the administration of the Great or City Dionysia held in honour of Dionysos of Eleutherai between the tenth and sixteenth or seventeenth days of Elaphebolion. Yet it was these two officials who ultimately were responsible for 'giving a chorus' to the playwrights who applied for one, and so deciding whether Aristophanes' latest would or would not be staged. Presumably they usually took advice or stuck with the familiar, which may explain Aristophanes' hiding behind the name of Kallistratos when he was just an unknown boy (see Brief 'Life', above).

Their next task was to appoint *khorēgoi* for each of the playwrights selected, usually five each for tragedy and comedy at the Dionysia, possibly reduced to three each for financial reasons during part of the Peloponnesian War. Certainly, right at the end of that war we hear of joint *khorēgiai*. This device was doubtless intended to diminish the financial burden or stimulate the flagging national spirit of the super-rich top few per cent of Athenians and resident aliens who were obligated by law to perform this *leitourgia* or 'national service'.

On the liberality or meanness of his *khorēgos* the success or failure of a playwright could perhaps depend – so Aristophanes humorously (we hope) intimated when he guyed the meanness of Antimakhos (*Acharnians* 1154-5). For the impresario paid for all the costumes, possibly both for frog-outfits (if the frog-chorus was visible) and for the initiates' rags in *Frogs*. He found and paid the twenty-four chorus-members, the *aulētēs* (player of the *aulos*, a kind of oboe), and perhaps also – except in Aristophanes' last two extant comedies, where the chorus part was severely curtailed – a specialist chorus-master. It was presumably he too who paid for any special effects required; and when the performance was over, especially if 'his' playwright had won, he was expected to provide a slap-up meal for all concerned. All this was expensive and could be hugely expensive. One impresario, for instance, claimed that in 403/2 he had expended 1600 drachmas, enough to keep five Athenian families of four alive at subsistence level for a year. In return, though, such lavish expenditure bought honour and prestige even in egalitarian Athens – and perhaps sometimes leniency from a People's court of jurors not known for their tenderness towards the idle and subversive rich (see chapter 5).

The playwrights and impresarios having been chosen, it only remained for the relevant official to select by lot the actors. Or rather perhaps they just selected the leading actor, who with the playwright chose the usually three or four supporting players. All actors were generically *hypokritai*, literally 'answerers' (whence our 'hypocrite'), because originally the one 'actor' had answered the chorus. But the three chief actors were also named respectively the *prōtagōnistēs*, *deuteragōnistēs*, and *tritagōnistēs*, because they were the first, second or third to conduct the *agōn* or argument (literally 'contest') of the play (see further, chapter 2). Between the protagonists, as between the playwrights and their *khorēgoi*, there was a competition with a prize. Indeed, because of this crucial competitive element in the Lenaia and Great Dionysia the whole festival could be called an *agōn*, a characteristically Greek twist. (For some reason we award prizes at film festivals, e.g. Cannes, but not at drama festivals, e.g. Edinburgh.) But who were to act as judges?

The answer, in a sense, is the audience, especially in comedy, where the playwrights went to great lengths to capture its benevolence by drawing it into the action, now flattering it grossly, now abusing it with tongue in cheek, even getting the chorus to shower spectators with nuts and other edible goodies. In return the audience didn't just laugh but applauded, hissed, booed, drummed the wooden benches with their heels, or called out as the fancy took them. The unrecoverable atmosphere of the occasion was perhaps something like a compound of being at a Christmas panto, in a thronged mediaeval Cathedral on Easter Day, and at a local football derby over the New Year holiday.

However, audience reaction, though obviously considered important, was not formally decisive by itself. The decision was entrusted instead to a small panel of judges appointed well in advance. Democratic principles, in other words, were not taken to the lengths they were in the Assembly, where the vote of each attender was taken into consideration. Rather, for the judging of tragedy and comedy, at any rate at the Dionysia, ten judges were selected, one representing each of the ten 'tribes' into which the whole citizen body was divided on a geographical basis. Even so, it appears that not every judge's vote might in the event be taken into consideration. By an elaborate – and to us obscure – procedure designed to eliminate the possibility of bribery or favouritism, only some of the ten judges' votes were actually counted. In *Frogs*, where an incompetent as well as incontinent Dionysos was made to judge between the claims of Aeschylus and Euripides, Aristophanes humorously contrived to suggest that all judging was an irrational, hit-or-miss affair.

Fairness, however, mattered less than the principles of open competition before and public judgment by one's peers, who were deemed to stand for the civic community as a whole. For comic drama was a product of the sovereign Athenian *polis*, part of a great state occasion that was organised by the people's own allotted representatives and financed both by the city from the public coffers and by rich individuals. It was staged in the context of a mass gathering that brought together hundreds of the citizens as active participants and many thousands as an involved audience. It was a crucial ingredient of a vital political event and an indispensable religious ritual.

We live in what we are pleased to call a democracy. But nothing, I think, could better illustrate the essential differences between British representative democracy in AD 1990 and Athenian direct, participatory democracy in 405 BC than a comparison between, say, a performance of *Henry V* at the National Theatre in London before a socially, economically and culturally privileged audience and the original performance of the *Frogs* in the Theatre of Dionysos at Athens before a mass audience of engaged citizens participating in a civic religio-political festival.

Fig. 4. Silver drachma of Sicilian Naxos: reverse depicts bunch of grapes hanging between vine-leaves, obverse (not shown) a head of Dionysos god of wine.

Chapter 2
Aristophanes' Idea of the Theatre

The idea of a theatre

It is striking just how many words in our everyday speech are metaphors derived ultimately from the theatre: person (persona, personality), scene, role, drama, stage, even theatre (as in 'political theatre'), among others. Clearly we find theatre a 'natural' sort of human activity, 'part of the scenery of life', we might say. Yet further reflection will reveal that, although most known human societies have produced and perhaps could not have functioned without some kind of dramatic representations (especially during rituals of passage from one status in life to another, e.g. initiation into adulthood), formalised theatre with its appropriate professional paraphernalia is a relatively late development, possible only in certain kinds of societies at certain levels of evolution and sophistication. Our contemporary, 'western' idea of the theatre, for example, is no older than the fifth or at most sixth century BC, since it had its origins in the theatre of ancient Athens.

One living token of this is that our word 'theatre' has an ancient Greek etymology. It is derived from *theatron*, which, as we saw in chapter 1, meant originally a group of spectators (*theatai*) and then by transference the space within which they watched (or rather participated in) the staged drama. However, it is important not to be seduced by this linguistic affiliation into assuming that 'theatre' carried exactly the same connotations in the collective mentality of the ancient Athenians as it does for us. Better, rather, to go to the opposite – if also exaggerated – extreme with Professor John Jones, who in his useful book *On Aristotle and Greek Tragedy* maintained that all ancient Greek drama, but especially tragedy, is 'desperately foreign' or irreducibly alien to our ways of seeing, thinking, and perceiving.

For the fact is that, just as the ancient Greeks invented our idea of competitive sports within the to us wholly alien context of a religious festival (that of Zeus Olympios at Olympia), so they pioneered our idea of theatre within the equally alien framework of the festival of

11

Dionysos Eleuthereus (chapter 1). This similarity in difference must be kept firmly in mind throughout this chapter, since when dealing with the theatricality and stagecraft of Aristophanes it is often necessary to speak of them as though Aristophanes were a present-day actor-manager working out of, say, London's Shaftesbury Avenue.

Old Comedy or Aristophanes?

The state of the surviving evidence is such that Old Comedy appears almost to have sprung fully formed from the brain and stylus of Aristophanes. But it should not be forgotten that he *did* have predecessors, and indeed contemporaries and rivals. What the ancient critics called 'Old Comedy' (to distinguish it from the 'New Comedy' of Menander; 'Middle Comedy' is a more recent and fuzzier classification) was not identical with the output of Aristophanes.

For a start, comedy as a genre had been officially recognised at the Dionysia since 486, forty years or so before Aristophanes was born, and at the Lenaia since about 440. When he made his debut in 427, comedy was almost sixty years old. Krates and Magnes were the great names of the first generation of comic playwrights; and Kratinos, a much older contemporary of Aristophanes who was showing before Aristophanes was born, yet survived many trials and tribulations to defeat the younger man's *Clouds* with his *Putinē* ('Flask') at the Dionysia of 423. Then there was his almost exact contemporary Eupolis, who kept pace with him until his death in 412/11. It is well, therefore, to repeat catechetically Horace's neat hexameter line *Eupolis atque Cratinus Aristophanesque poetae* ('Eupolis and Cratinus and Aristophanes poets...'), in order to put Aristophanes' achievement in its proper perspective.

All the same, it does seem pretty clear that the contribution of Aristophanes to comedy was overwhelming and unique, that it was he above all who shaped the genre of Old Comedy and set the standards by which all those comedians who 'asked for a chorus' had to be judged. The pity is that he was so successful, first with a succession of 'King' and Eponymous Archons and a string of audiences in his lifetime and then with scholars and copyists after his death, that there is virtually nothing left of his predecessors' or contemporaries' work to judge his by. Even of Aristophanes, of course, we only have about one quarter of his original output in anything like its original form, and the remainder of the almost 400 known plays survive only in snippety quotations or tatters of papyrus fragments or just as bare titles. This largely irremediable incompleteness inevitably weakens the force of any generalisation we would want to make about any aspect of Aristophanes' comic theatre. But that is not by any means the most serious impediment to our understanding and appreciation.

Material props and production values

Ancient Greek *drama* means literally 'something done', and progressive modern commentators are agreed that a purely or predominantly text-based approach to Aristophanes is fatally skewed. Yet not only are the cultural context and audience-mentality for Athenian comic drama 'desperately foreign' but we can also never precisely recover the physical, audio-visual elements of the original performances, even – or especially – when the plays are put on today in an ancient Greek theatre such as the magnificently preserved example at Epidauros in the Peloponnese. The theatrical setting, the costumes, the movements, gestures and delivery of the actors, the singing and dancing of the chorus, the musical score, above all the sense of occasion – these have all gone, for good. Hence of course the privileging of the evidence provided directly by the extant texts, but hence too the over-intellectual quality of much modern study of them. The balance should be redressed: before literary or any other criticism of the subtleties and beauties of the texts may legitimately be conducted, the physical scene of the dramas must be set by reconstructing something at least of their external manifestations, what I have called their material props.

For a start the harmonious proportions and finely-dressed masonry of the theatre at Epidauros must be thought away. So too must the remains of the mainly Roman-period stone-built theatre that confront the modern visitor to the Theatre of Dionysos in Athens. The first stone theatre on the latter site was not constructed until half a century or so after the death of Aristophanes. *His* theatre was a much more makeshift and less grandiose affair. Correspondingly the wider geographical setting of the theatre was that much more important to him.

The shrine or sanctuary (*temenos*) of Dionysos Eleuthereus of which the theatral area formed a part was situated on the south-east slope of the Acropolis ('High City') hill. The Acropolis dominated Aristophanes' Athens far more than it does the high-rise centre of

Fig. 5. Theatre of Dionysos, Roman period. View from south wall of Acropolis.

modern urban Athens: for example, Herodotus could liken Athens to a wheel whose hub was the Acropolis hill. This was a doubly appropriate site for Dionysiac drama. Not only was the Acropolis the focus of Athenian religious and other civic activity but it was also suitable geophysically. The abrupt rock of the hill itself afforded shelter from the nippy north winds that can blow during January/ February and March/April when the Lenaia and Dionysia festivals fell due, while the lower slope of the hill could be specially prepared for acoustic and visual purposes to accommodate superimposed rows of seating – in Aristophanes' day just earthen banking and wooden benches – for perhaps some 14-15,000 spectators. From their benches or the ground they looked down on the drama and beyond it to the plain that stretched to Mount Hymettos and the Aegean Sea. The whole geographical setting, in other words, including the very daylight, was drawn into the dramatic scene rather than excluded or obliterated. Nothing could be further removed from the enclosed space and artificial lighting of our modern theatre buildings.

The drama itself took place in a prepared area at the foot of the hill. The origins of comedy, as we saw (chapter 1), are obscure, but it is agreed that it somehow grew out of ritual miming, singing and above all dancing (*khoros* meant basically 'dance') – actions and words that told or burlesqued stories relevant to the Athenians' everyday religious and political experience. Thus the essential component of the theatre was the circular dancing-floor of beaten earth (perhaps modelled on the threshing-floor) known as the *orkhēstra*. Here the Chorus of twenty-four masked men representing humans, animals or personifications chanted in unison the lyric passages which served – at least until Aristophanes dropped them some time after *Frogs* – as *entr'actes*, and danced mimetically their carefully choreographed steps to the accompaniment of a single instrument something like an oboe (*aulos*).

The three, four or sometimes more actors were also men wearing masks (*prosōpa*, but probably never *portrait* masks), together with grotesquely padded clothing and phallos where appropriate. They occupied a separately defined space behind the *orkhēstra*, a raised but still low wooden stage to which they gained access from the *skēnē*. The latter word means literally 'tent', 'booth' or 'hut', but Aristophanes' *skēnē* seems to have been a rectangular, roofed building of light wooden construction. It served both as the actors' dressing-room and mask-changing room and as the main prop, a house or houses for house or houses for example, with one or more doors.

Those, then, are the bare material bones of all Aristophanic comedy: let us begin now to surround them with the flesh, blood and guts of an actual play, the *Thesmophoriazusae*. If the usual interpretation is right, this was staged at the Dionysia of 411, a couple of months after *Lysistrata*. The feverish activity that must have been involved for Aristophanes in producing two plays in a single year matched the mounting tension of the political atmosphere in Athens on the eve of the outbreak of civil violence and bloody oligarchic counter-revolution in the summer of that year. It is hard to believe that the two were not connected.

Structure, plot and theme of Thesmophoriazusae

It seems foolish to speak of the 'traditional structure of Old Comedy' when Aristophanes' comedy is virtually all we have to go on, but it would appear that he either inherited or created such a structure, which he also both occasionally varied and permanently modified.

(a) Prologue

The actors enter and perform a series of skits or routines, often farcical and by no means always relevant to the succeeding plot, which they introduce along with themselves in preparation for the entry of the chorus. In *Thesmophoriazusae* Euripides enters with an elderly male relative (often called Mnesilokhos, the name of the real Euripides' father-in-law). He reveals that the respectable married women of Athens are exploiting the cover of their three-day women-only Thesmophoria festival (held during the month Pyanopsion, October/November) to hold an assembly 'with a view to his [Euripides'] destruction'. Their reason? Euripides' grossly unfavourable representation of legendary women in his tragedies, which has given *all* women a bad name.

Euripides' first wheeze is to try, with the aid of his Relative, to persuade another tragic poet, Agathon, to smuggle himself in drag into the women's assembly so as to put the case for Euripides' defence. At one theatrical stroke Aristophanes has allowed himself to swipe at Euripides' alleged misogyny and Agathon's alleged effeminacy, to parody both their tragic styles and tragic drama as such, and to set up the beguilingly authentic impossibility of an encounter between a male actor playing an effeminate male tragedian in drag and a Chorus of male actors impersonating women in a supposedly secret, women-only religious ritual in front of a possibly all-male (though not all-Athenian) audience. Agathon, however, cannot be persuaded, so the thoroughly masculine Relative volunteers to go in his place – and clothes. But getting the Relative properly made up for the part of female impersonator is a messier job. For of course even his genital area (in fact either invisible or distinguished unambiguously by his comic phallos) has to be shaved – or rather singed: cue for some boisterous slapstick. One final paratragic comic device ends the Prologue, the wheeling out (*ekkyklēma*) of Agathon on the trolley used in tragedy to show murdered corpses.

(b) Parodos
At last – in *Thesmophoriazusae* after more than 300 lines (perhaps some twenty minutes) – the Chorus enters and the main action normally begins. A conflict develops, often between the actors on one side and the Chorus on the other. The scene has shifted to the Thesmophoria – in imagination only: this is a theatre of convention, not illusion in the modern, naturalistic sense, and there is no attempt to use different scenery or props to suggest the real Thesmophoria setting. The Relative mingles with the Chorus of celebrants and the women who will have speaking roles (in all, the play requires four actors), as they inaugurate their assembly with a nice mixture of near-genuine prayer- and curse-formulae borrowed from the male citizen Assembly held on the Pnyx hill and topical references to Euripides and the presumedly secret vices of women.

(c) Agōn
The 'contest' involves a stylised alternation of speeches and songs which always includes the breath-catching, tongue-twisting patter-song called *pnigos* ('choking'). Anonymous women speakers and the Chorus battle it out with the old Relative, who raises the temperature and the roof by trumping even Euripides' slanderous accusations against the female sex. These the women denounce, not as untrue, but as disloyal, before they are saved from even worse by the timely intervention of Kleisthenes, who like Agathon is presented as effeminate and thus in context as an honorary woman. In a parody of a Euripidean *anagnōrisis* (recognition scene) and amid one of the bawdiest routines in all surviving Aristophanes, the old Relative is caught, 'unmasked', and placed under female guard.

(d) Parabasis

The Chorus comes forward (*parabainei*, hence *parabasis*) for the Leader to offer what sounds like serious advice of a political nature – that is, on some general political principle or particular political issue of the day. Often, as in *Frogs*, this advice is unconnected with anything else in the play, but in *Thesmophoriazusae* it is of course entirely apropos for the Chorus of Athenian wives to 'turn to the People, our own panegyric to render' because 'Men never speak a good word, never one, for the feminine gender' (trans. B.B. Rogers), and then to contrast the honesty, hard work and thrift of women in their homes with the dishonest public graft of male political leaders like Kleophon. Just how seriously this advice was meant by Aristophanes and taken by his audience, or how seriously we should take it today, is of course a different question, to which we shall return in various connections.

(e) Consequences of the agōn

To the *parabasis* succeeds a sequence of self-contained sketches and scenes of farce through which the consequences of the *agōn* are worked out. In *Thesmophoriazusae* the leitmotif of this section continues the theme of disguise and recognition. Euripides, honouring his oath to help his Relative if need be, appears successively as characters in his own tragedies (Menelaos and Perseus), reciting or singing the appropriate paratragic verses (tragic language, tone and gesture incongruously placed in a comic setting). A new ingredient is stirred into the humorous mix-up with the introduction of one of Athens' regular policemen, a Scythian slave-archer (one of the thousand or so owned by the community). The scope for misunderstanding, especially linguistic, is fully exploited, and despite or because of Euripides' efforts the Relative remains in police custody.

(f) Exodos

In the 'departure' the plot, which is developed with unusual consistency in *Thesmophoriazusae*, reaches its climax, and the contest is finally resolved, frequently (though not in *Thesmophoriazusae*) with the performance of some such suitably joyful and carnivalesque celebration as a wedding. Having failed to persuade the Scythian to release his Relative by means of pseudo-intellectual word-mongering, Euripides resorts to the more earthy charms of sex. After the Chorus

has sung a beautiful hymn to Athena (patron of Athens) and Demeter
and Persephone (patrons of the Thesmophoria), he finally returns
disguised as an old woman bringing with 'her' two attractive young
girls, a piper and a dancer. While the ithyphallic policeman takes his
necessarily fleeting pleasure with the dancing girl (offstage – as always
in Greek theatre), Euripides and his Relative make their escape,
aided by the now complaisant Chorus ('they went thataway' – pointing
in the opposite direction). The latter has been reconciled to Euripides
by his promise to make no more 'revelations' about the foibles of their
sex, to return male-female relations to 'business as usual'. The play
concludes with the Chorus' anticipating their return home to
domestic bliss and counting on 'The Two' (Demeter and Persephone)
to 'bless with success our performance today'.

Aristophanes' artful craft

Thesmophoriazusae has rightly, and with aptly Aristophanic
paronomasia, been described as 'a play on worlds' (Nick Lowe in
Omnibus 17). In the perhaps more typically patterned plays like
Acharnians the hero is a 'little man' who conceives a 'big idea' to
transform (almost) single-handed some global situation that he finds
intolerable. The ordinariness of the starting-point is crucial to the
comedy, since it provides the necessary flipside to the surrealist
fantasy, inconsequentiality and suspension of normal causality that
characterise what might laughingly be called the development of the
plot. In *Thesmophoriazusae*, however, not only is there a recognisable
and internally coherent plot-line but the intrinsic humour of the plot
is of a markedly more sophisticated nature, approximated only by that
of *Ecclesiazusae*, which takes further the implications of a parliament
of women (chapter 4).

   For it depends on the consistent blurring of boundaries within
'this' world rather than a definitive take-off from one kind of world
into another. Thus we find confused or transgressed the following
natural or conventional boundaries: between real life and fiction (the
'real' Euripides and the 'stage-stereotype' Euripides, for instance –
this fooled at least one post-Classical biographer of Euripides!),
between men's lives and women's lives, and between high (tragic) and
low (comic) art. These perhaps rather cerebral transgressions were
brilliantly transposed into a more immediately accessible key by way
of a series of devices: literary and linguistic parody (no less than two
thirds of the play consists of paratragedy), multiple cross-dressing

(male actors playing effeminate male characters in feminine attire, male actors playing conventionally masculine men disguised as women, male actors playing conventionally feminine women), and a great variety of impersonations that placed particularly heavy demands on the vocal dexterity and (panto)miming skills of the actor who played the Relative (one of the three 'meatiest' of known Aristophanic roles, along with Philokleon in *Wasps* and Dionysos in *Frogs*).

Some commentators have depreciated *Thesmophoriazusae* as a 'literary' play without a serious point or message. Leaving on one side for the moment the general problem of whether *any* Aristophanic play can be said to be serious in this sense, it seems to me that in his close engagement with Euripides (not confined to this play, as we have seen) Aristophanes was being as deadly serious as he ever could be; because what was at stake was nothing less than his art which for him was his life. Euripides – the playwright, not the man – bothered him greatly for several reasons, but most of all, I believe, because his art was uncomfortably like his own. Euripides, in a word, was too comic.

His *Ion* was a tragedy in the comic mode; in *Elektra* he burlesqued an Aeschylean recognition scene; he innovated by his references to food and drink and other mundane 'domestic goods and chattels' (*Frogs* 959-60); he 'democratised' tragedy by making Elektra's husband a peasant farmer of even lower socio-economic status than, say, Trygaios in *Peace* and by giving greater prominence to slaves, children, old nurses, and minor characters; he reduced his choruses to singing vacuous lyrics without deeper implication either for the action or for the religious and moral dimensions of his drama; and so on. Kratinos was hitting the mark when he invented the word *euripidaristophanizein* to suggest a certain similarity of approach. But the sting in that compound verb lay in the fact that no tragic poet formally wrote comedy or vice versa; indeed, from one point of view comedy was precisely not-tragedy, or tragedy through the looking glass. So by travestying 'Euripides' himself in *Thesmophoriazusae*, Aristophanes was – mildly, to be sure – getting his own back, standing up for the Comic Muse against her older Tragic sister, protesting silently against the arrangement of the Dionysia programme which always put comedy on last each day, after the tragedies and satyr-plays.

But that in itself would not have been terribly funny, and whatever else the comic playwright might do or want to do he had by hook or by crook to make his audience laugh and go away happy. For us, though, this poses a major problem. To discover where Aristophanes does or does not intend to be funny when we have only the text to go on is hard enough in itself. But to comprehend the humour, including the sense of humour, of an alien culture is even harder. And this is a 'major' problem, because knowing what a culture finds funny and how it uses laughter socially is an indispensable part of understanding that culture. Fortunately, a good deal of the 'broader' Aristophanic humour does travel – the slapstick, the farce, much of the bawdy and obscenity, the grotesque satire. So too the literary parody (at least where we have the parodied original) and ingenious verbal play can often be grasped and appreciated. But the humour of tone, gesture and movement is largely lost. We can never be sure that we have really picked up all or even most of the *double* (or more) *entendres*, and many topical political allusions are to us – as perhaps to some of the audience – utterly opaque.

Happily, from this standpoint, *Thesmophoriazusae* is remarkably free from vitriolic personal abuse and obscure topical political allusion and does illustrate most of the main types of Aristophanic humour. The slapstick of the shaving routine, the bawdy of the unmasking scene, and the relentless verbal paratragedy have already been mentioned. The humour of the Scythian policeman's fractured speech, sadly, was probably racist, since that was the sort of pidgin Attic Greek such 'wogs' probably did actually speak. Similarly, the humour in the jokes about women's allegedly incontinent passion for booze and sex was very likely sexist, reflecting and projecting real-life Athenian men's anxieties and women's frustrations in these two crucial domains of male chauvinist domination (cf. chapter 4). On the technical side we have already noted the doubly paratragic *ekkyklēma* of Agathon; the equally paratragic use of the crane (*Thesmophoriazusae* 1099-100), burlesquing Euripides' lost *Andromeda*, also deserves mention. All in all, what we have in *Thesmophoriazusae* is a satisfyingly complete piece of Aristophanic theatre.

Chapter 3
The Wisdom of the Poet

A rare dramatic failure or a roaring success?

After a run of two first prizes at successive Lenaia, Aristophanes in 423 tried his hand again at the Dionysia, where he may have won three years earlier with *Babylonians*. Sadly, *Clouds* (*Nephelai*) was a flop and came third, beaten both by Kratinos' swansong play *Putinē* and by Ameipsias' *Konnos*. It is usually impossible for us to say why a play did – or did not – win. The generosity or meanness of the impresario, the quality of the actor allotted to the playwright as protagonist, the order in which the three comic plays were performed, the vagaries of the judging procedure – these and other external factors could have had as much to do with the result as the intrinsic merits of the play's theme and treatment, let alone any 'message' the play may have been thought to express (e.g. in the *parabasis*). In the case of *Clouds*, however, we have a little more to go on.

In the *parabasis* of the play as we have it, the Chorus – speaking as normal in the authorial first person – bitterly lament the play's fate at the hands of the judges:

> Dear spectators, freely shall I speak to you, yes and truly,
> So help me Dionysus, whose ward I am. So surely may I win,
> So surely be deemed a poet, as I reckon you a clever audience
> And this the best of my plays. Much labor has it cost me,
> And I thought you'd approve it, but I retired defeated,
> Most unfairly, by clumsy rivals. 'Tis you I blame, the clever,
> For whose sake I took such pains...

> (trans. Moses Hadas, ll. 518-26)

It was normal for a comic poet to appeal for the audience's benevolence and not unheard of for him mock-seriously to abuse them. But it was not normal for the *parabasis* of a play that was performed just once to refer unambiguously in the past tense to the play's fate with the judges; and the tone of the abuse has an edge to it that suggests more than the customary jocular banter. To reveal all:

Fig. 6. Socrates.

those quoted lines at any rate did not belong to the original stage presentation of *Clouds* but were inserted into the revised, second edition of the play – an edition that was put into circulation as a text perhaps some five years after. Thus whereas Aristophanes wrote two *different* plays entitled *Thesmophoriazusae* and two entitled *Plutus*, his two *Clouds* were but different versions of the *same* play.

It would at first sight seem to be a fair inference from the fact of rewriting that Aristophanes attributed at least some of the blame for the play's failure to his own script. However, although the people who perhaps bought but anyway read *Clouds* Mark II may have also most of them seen the Mark I version in 423, they will have constituted a tiny, and socio-economically grossly unrepresentative sample of that original audience. So Aristophanes' motive or motives in circulating a revised text must have been somehow different from those which lay behind the original theatrical presentation of the play.

I shall return to what those motives may have been later. Now I want us to jump ahead in imagination some twenty years, to the fraught period of Athenian history after defeat in the Peloponnesian War, imposition of a vicious oligarchic junta and restoration of democracy, all at the behest or under the aegis of the new Greek superpower, Sparta. A 'general amnesty' was technically in force at Athens, which legally prohibited public muckraking of any sort that involved reference to a man's alleged implication in oligarchic counter-revolution during or immediately after the war. But in the years around 400 half a dozen major public trials were held (or perhaps we should say 'staged') which in spirit if not in the letter breached the amnesty. One of these, the most famous today, was the trial in 399 of Socrates, former teacher or intimate associate of notorious oligarchs, who was accused of impiety and corrupting the young.

Socrates himself, who apparently never wrote a word of his philosophy for permanent record, naturally did not write a formal defence-speech. Nor did he commission one, as he could have done, from a professional speechwriter. But after his condemnation and execution two of his outraged pupils wrote one for him, of which the *Apology* (*apologia* means 'defence speech') of Plato is much the better known. If we are to believe Plato's *Apology*, it was in 399 that *Clouds* scored its greatest success. For 'Socrates' is made to claim that Aristophanes' presentation of him had seriously prejudiced Athenian popular opinion against him.

We cannot, unfortunately, know whether the real Socrates did actually refer to *Clouds* in 399; elsewhere, in the *Symposium* (dramatic date 416, i.e. seven years after the performance of *Clouds*), Plato could present Aristophanes and Socrates as amicably sharing the pleasures of an all-male upper-class intellectual drinking-party (*symposion*) held to celebrate a victory at the Lenaia won by the tragic poet Agathon (see previous chapter). But it certainly was true that in delivering judgment an Athenian jury was as much influenced by its perception of the defendant's career as a whole and moral-political impact on the community in general as it was by the 'facts' of the specific charge before it; and Plato's wider implication that art and life were easily confused in Athens should not surprise us after our discussion of the *Thesmophoriazusae*. What interests me here, though, is not Socrates' or Plato's but Aristophanes' view of 'his' Socrates in *Clouds*.

New paideia for old

First, the wider intellectual or rather educational context of the play must be considered. The Greek for 'education' was *paideia*, because it was a matter for *paides* or children. But *paideia* and *paideusis* (process of education) had a broader, metaphorical application too, as when in the Funeral Speech Pericles hymned Athens' democratic way of life as 'an education (*paideusis*) for all Greece'. For the Greeks, in other words, education was not just a technical term for what went on in school but a moral concern of the community embracing the dealings of a public civic courtroom no less than those of a private classroom.

Most Athenian male children were taught the rudiments of literacy, numeracy and music, and most of those were taught them outside the home by one or more professional teachers. (The education of Athenian girls was another matter, usually left to their mother, assisted perhaps by a literate household slave.) But although the city was committed to its citizens' *paideia*, Athens did not provide a state-run education system. Since formal education was an entirely private affair, financial circumstances dictated its quality and duration, both of which therefore were for most Athenians pretty minimal. There was nothing corresponding to our notion of 'secondary' education, for example. But all of a sudden, beginning in the third quarter of the fifth century BC, Athenian fathers were presented with the possibility of 'tertiary' or 'higher level' education for their sons. Or rather, realistically speaking, only *some* of them were, because this new source of formal instruction did not come cheap.

It was provided by teachers who were mostly itinerant and not themselves Athenian by birth. They came to be called collectively *sophistai* or Sophists with a capital 'S', even though their doctrines and teaching methods were not uniform and they did not form a philosophical or any other kind of school. Because very little indeed of their original writings has survived, and because we learn about them in the main from their often very bitter enemies, the Sophists have generally had a bad press and been classed pejoratively as 'sophistical' (rather than sophisticated) thinkers and teachers, masters of linguistic dirty tricks, and cynical purveyors of immoral techniques of argument. The *Clouds*, in which 'Socrates' is made to stand for this class of teacher, has had a great influence in impressing this unfavourable image of the Sophists on posterity – indeed, almost as much as Plato, except that Plato of course went to enormous lengths to differentiate his revered master Socrates from the unspeakable Sophists.

Why, then, did Aristophanes feel that the new *paideia* of the Sophists was a suitable subject for comedy, that is comic vilification, in 424/3, and why did he choose to satirise Socrates as the emblematic spokesman of this supposedly pernicious educational movement? The second question is the easier to answer. The language of abuse at Athens – not just comic abuse, but the more narrowly political abuse in the lawcourts or Assembly, say – was always personal, reducing general issues to matters of individual personality. For his incarnation of the evils of Sophistry Aristophanes needed some instantly recognisable public figure, and Socrates (then aged 46) must have seemed heaven-sent.

Firstly, he was an Athenian, and although the *Clouds* was presented at the more international Dionysia festival, Aristophanes' primary target was as ever the Athenian component of the audience. Secondly, in his physical appearance Socrates resembled nothing so much as the satyrs familiar to the audience from sculpture and vase-painting and, more relevantly, the immediately preceding satyr-play. No less than the playwright, the mask-makers will have enjoyed playing on the confusion between the real-world Socrates and the sati/yrical 'Socrates' of *Clouds*. Thirdly, and most importantly, Socrates' circle of pupils was drawn from the class of Athenian 'notables' and significantly included the notorious Alcibiades, relative and former ward of Pericles, friend and probably junior sexual partner of Socrates, whom Aristophanes had already had a go at in his maiden *Banqueters* when Alcibiades was in his early twenties. This was the 'pin-up' or 'pop-star' brigade of democratic Athens, about whom ordinary Athenians were most anxious to hear.

But what of our other question, the relevance of Sophistry as a vehicle for Aristophanes' comedy? His very first comedy *Banqueters* had had as its theme precisely the question of the 'new education'. In the same year as that was performed the famous Sicilian Greek Sophist Gorgias had spoken before the Athenian Assembly on behalf of his city of Leontinoi – to miraculous effect. The audience had been bedazzled by his rhetoric and persuaded by his appeal. That same summer, if Thucydides is to be believed, Kleon during a major debate over public policy (how to deal with the imperial Athenians' revolted Mytilenaian subjects) had castigated the Assembly for their willingness to listen to and be influenced by public debating contests put on as sideshows by rival Sophists. By 427, then, the connection between Sophistry, rhetoric and public political success had become plain. The underlying reason for the connection was, in a word, democracy: the shift of political power to mass meetings of ordinary citizens (the *dēmos*) in Assembly and lawcourts who had the power (*kratos*) to make decisions of state on behalf of the *polis*. Persuasion thereby acquired a premium value in the city of words, and the political and material rewards for any 'orator' (*rhētōr*, which was also used to mean 'politician') who could deliver the persuasive goods were enormous. So too were the rewards for those who could teach the necessary skills: which is where the Sophists came in.

And also where Aristophanes joins the debate. We have already noticed his early comic interest in the 'educational question'. In 423 that interest was given a specifically political slant by way of 'Socrates' and his supposed thought-reform school. The degree and nature of the interest emerge most clearly when *Clouds* is set within the developing sequence of Aristophanes' political preoccupations: *Babylonians* – the character of the Athenian Empire; *Acharnians* – interstate relations; *Knights* – democratic decision-making in the Assembly; *Clouds* – persuasive rhetoric and public moral values; *Wasps* – democratic decision-making in the popular jurycourts; *Peace* – interstate relations again. The *Clouds*, in other words, is a topical political play in the sense that Aristophanes was then powerfully engaged by the phenomenon of mass power. The positioning of *Clouds* within his *oeuvre*, together with his 'publishing' of a second, written edition, suggest that his engagement was more than purely humorous.

Vortex rules O.K.?

In modern Greek *phrontistērion* means 'crammer' or (more genteelly) 'tutorial college'. In Aristophanic Greek it meant literally the 'Thinkery' (or, more topically for us, 'Think Tank' or, perhaps, 'Blaboratory') presided over by the scientifically speculative, religiously sceptical, venal, dishonest, workshy and cynical Socrates. This was where old Strepsiades ('Twister'), a rustic who'd married above himself into the urban, horsey Athenian aristocracy (another link with *Knights*), took the notion of sending his son Pheidippides (named for the distaff side of the family), in order to help him wriggle out of repaying the debts his horse-fancying son's expensive tastes had saddled him with. Unlike the pattern followed in several Aristophanic plays, this can hardly be described as a 'great idea' of the 'little man' hero, since Strepsiades' personal and rather squalid financial affairs are hardly on an equality of global significance with the troubles caused by the Peloponnesian War. Aristophanes, it would seem, was much more interested in the implications, humorous or otherwise, of Socrates' Phrontisterion.

Pheidippides, however, in this as in other matters, is not the dutiful son of Athenian unwritten law and refuses to enrol. So Strepsiades feels constrained to find out in person whether this old dog can be taught the new Socratic tricks of rhetoric and is duly enrolled by Socrates himself, in a parody of ritual initiation. The point of this is to introduce the important religious sub-theme of the plot. For the school's divine patrons are the eponymous Clouds (a brilliant Aristophanic idea which enables him to make play with the agricultural blessings that will be conferred on Strepsiades if he proves a model student, echoing the blessings genuinely promised to, for example, devotees of the Eleusinian Mysteries), and yet the Phrontisterion is really a hotbed of irreligion or at least unlicensed religion. According to strict scientific principles it is proven to Strepsiades that it is not Zeus who is the master of the universe, but Dinos ('Vortex' – cue for a visual pun, since *dinos* also meant a certain shape of pot).

Alas, Strepsiades does not turn out to be a model student; in particular, he fails to take on board the school's high-minded and ascetic moral ideals and is summarily expelled. Putting the screws on Pheidippides again, he does this time persuade his delinquent son to sign on with Socrates. But before Pheidippides' instruction begins Strepsiades is offered a choice of tuition, presented – in a mockery of the Sophistic contests derided by the Thucydidean Kleon (above) – in the form of a debate between Dikaios Logos ('Just' or 'Right' Argument) and Adikos ('Unjust' or 'Wrong') Logos. In the original presentation the rival Arguments were portrayed 'fighting like birds, in wicker cages', and a vase of the period showing two men dressed as fighting cocks could be an actual illustration of this. Needless to say, Adikos Logos emerges triumphant by making his worse or weaker argument seem better or stronger, Pheidippides duly studies the Worse way, and Strepsiades routs two creditors with his second-hand (and of course garbled) learning.

But Aristophanes is not finished with the practical implications of the new education. For it turns out that Pheidippides has not only assimilated verbal debating-tricks, mere techniques, but also imbibed newfangled tastes and values in poetry, finding especially pleasing what his father considers the postmodernist immoralities of Euripides. When Pheidippides' answer to his father's remonstrations is to give a literal and distinctly unfilial interpretation of the famous Sophist Protagoras' work entitled 'Knock-down Arguments', an outraged Strepsiades helped by one of his slaves (yet another Xanthias or 'Blondy': see chapter 7) puts a match – or rather a brand – to the Phrontisterion in order to obliterate this accursed nest of public enemies. (At least he does so in our *Clouds*; the original version may have ended differently.)

In defence of poetry?

Among the gallery of plausible stereotypes that Aristophanes parades across his comic theatre there is one significant absentee: the poet as such. The 'philosopher' is there (Socrates), the 'politician' (Kleon aka the Paphlagonian slave in Knights: see chapter 5), the *miles gloriosus* (Lamakhos in *Acharnians*), and so on. But not the poet. Individual comic and tragic poets are of course abused or satirised, more or less good- or ill-naturedly, and tragedy as a genre is consistently sent up. But through all the plays runs a theme of not obviously comic invocation of the divinities and supernatural powers associated with all poetry, from Apollo and the Muses to the Graces (a grace-ful couplet attributed to Plato aptly maintained 'The Graces were looking for an everlasting home;/They found it in the soul of Aristophanes'). And when the chips were truly down in the real Athenian world of early 405, there was nothing intrinsically funny in the *Frogs'* governing idea that Dionysos should fetch back from Hades a tragic poet to save the city. (It had to be a *tragic* poet, not because Aristophanes conceded that tragedy was a more valuable public art-form than comedy, but because he could get more laughs out of tragedy and could not concede that there was any other suitable comic candidate for the job of poet-saviour of the city besides himself.) The basis of the poet's claim to offer advice and even salvation was his wisdom (*sophia*), and there, I suggest, lay the rub of the *Clouds*.

A *sophistēs* originally meant anyone whose claim to being *sophos*, to having practical wisdom, was widely accepted. Solon the early sixth-century BC lawgiver was perhaps the classic example of such a person in the minds of most fifth-century Athenians, and Solon had given his practical political advice interlarded with moral homily in verse. But *the* poet for Athenians, as for other Greeks, was of course Homer, and although it is misleading to speak of his work as the Greeks' equivalent of a Bible, it is not possible to overestimate the didactic impact of Homer on ordinary Greek consciousness and consciences – least of all at Athens, where his poetry was recited annually at the great birthday festival of Athena, the city's divine patron, the Panathenaia. Thus the notions of poetry and civic wisdom were inextricably intermingled in the popular mind – until the development of rhetoric associated with the Sophists, which expressed itself no longer in verse but in prose. Aristophanes therefore had more than a little personal and professional interest in giving Sophistry a bad name.

This gives peculiar significance to the strikingly repeated variations on *sophos* and cognate words in the *parabasis* specially composed for the circulated written text of *Clouds*. If he speaks the truth without restraint, he will be accounted *sophos* by the audience; *Clouds* was the 'wisest' of his plays, and it's the *sophoi* he blames for not giving it its due reward; he has written it for the *sophoi*, whom he reminds that he is always 'intellectualising' (*sophizomai*) brand-new ideas; and it is the 'wisest spectators' whom he again bids pay attention. In performance the apparent seriousness of these pleas might have been undercut by comic by-play, modulations of tone of voice, or other dramatic devices. In cold print (as it were) those deflating effects were unavailable, and it is hard to resist the idea that Aristophanes was doing with the *Clouds* what the oligarch Antiphon had pioneered with his written versions of forensic speeches, conducting politics by other, covert means.

This, I believe, is the spirit in which we should read (as distinct from that in which the original audiences heard and received) the pearls of didactic wisdom with which Aristophanes studded his extant plays: from *Acharnians* (500: 'even Comedy [*trugōidia*, punning on *trugē*, 'vintage'] knows what is right'), through *Frogs* (1054-6: just as children have tutors, so 'grown-ups have poets to teach them', according to 'Aeschylus', eventual winner of the contest for 'city-saviour'; 'Euripides' concurred, 1008-10), to *Ecclesiazusae* (1155-6: 'Let the wise and philosophic choose me for my wisdom's sake./Those who joy in mirth and laughter choose me for the jests I make', in B.B. Rogers' translation). In a sense the cynical rejoinder – well, he would say that, wouldn't he? – is utterly appropriate, because it does seem to have been one of comedy's functions to reassert and reaffirm within a festive context the traditional norms of society that tragedy and other forms of persuasive speech more fundamentally put at risk. But in view of the 'publication' of *Clouds* Mark II, it seems hard to maintain that that was all there was to Aristophanes' defence of poetic didacticism: methinks he did protest both too much and too often.

Chapter 4
The Women of Aristophanes

The monstrous regiment

A French scholar writing in the early 1960s thought he could detect 'a certain feminism', that is (according to a dictionary definition) advocacy of women's rights on the ground of the equality of women, in the literature of Athens in the years around 400 BC. Euripides' *Medea*, for instance, the women of the 'Guardian' class in Plato's *Republic*, and of course Aristophanes' eponymous Lysistrata and his Praxagora of *Ecclesiazusae*, not to mention Aspasia (Pericles' 'common law' wife in real life and frequent butt of the comic dramatists) – were not these all symptoms of a groundswell of feeling that women at Athens merited greater public visibility and responsibility? Since the rise of the contemporary women's movement in the later sixties, with its profound impact on academic scholarship and on politics and society generally, this approach has been taken a great deal further, as feminist scholars of both sexes have tried to rescue the silent women of Athens (almost none of whom speaks to us in her own right) from masculine condescension or oblivion. The result has been a far more balanced appreciation and understanding of Athenian society and mentality with a corresponding improvement in the writing of the general history of Athens.

Many problems, however, both theoretical and practical, remain. Is there a 'history of women', that is of women *separate from* and *as opposed to* men? Even if such a history might be conceivable or desirable theoretically, can it be put into practice with the evidence available? Since in the case of women at Athens the relevant evidence was written or otherwise produced almost entirely by and for men, is it possible to reconstruct and comprehend anything of women's lives behind and beyond the images of them (possibly idealised or in other ways distorted) constructed by men for male consumption? In these circumstances it is not difficult to see why there has been so much interest recently in the women of Aristophanes, who were of course fictional characters in comic plays but were also, unlike the non-Greek princess Medea, say, or the non-Athenian queen Clytemnestra, supposedly everyday Athenian women, 'girl-next-door' types.

Those interpreters of Aristophanes who refuse to take him or his work seriously, on the grounds that his invented characters are participating in an intrinsically fantastic carnival of licensed religious festivity and that his sole intention was to make the audience laugh so that he could win first prize, see no reason to share this interest. They point out that all the actors and chorus-members were male, and some of them anyway also believe that the audience too was entirely male. Aristophanes' women, therefore, in their view, have nothing to tell us about real Athenian women of the late fifth or early fourth century. At most they may somehow reflect male Athenian perceptions of them.

These interpreters are right to emphasise the carnival context of Aristophanic drama, which legitimated the playwright's take-off into inconsequential flights of absurdist fantasy, and right too to bring out the background of Athenian popular myth (especially myths about those dangerously androgynous females, the Amazons) which shaped his feminine dramatic creations. But they are wrong to ignore a crucial source of the humour in those fantastic flights of imagination, that is, Aristophanes' consciously incongruous juxtaposition of the everyday and the extraordinary. A central ingredient in the humour of Aristophanes' women, in other words, is the mingling of the commonplace with the absurd, the mythical with the down-to-earth, and it is the delicate task of balanced modern historical interpretation to try to disentangle the one from the other. Only then can we go on to see what purpose if any, beyond raising a laugh, Aristophanes may have had in foisting these creations on an unsuspecting public.

I stress 'unsuspecting'. The 'King' Archon and his 'editorial board', who 'gave a chorus' to Aristophanes for the *Lysistrata* to be performed at probably the Lenaia of 411 and for the *Ecclesiazusae*, probably at the Lenaia of 392, will have been offered some idea both of the plots and of their treatment. But the vast majority of the original audiences of these works will surely have gasped at the shock of the new. Not only is the *Lysistrata* one of only two of Aristophanes' extant comedies to take its name from the leading character, but unlike the other (*Plutus*) *Lysistrata* is named after an ordinary human character, not a god, and a female one to boot. This pioneering mode of titulature was presumably adopted because Lysistrata was, apparently, the first heroine in all Old Comedy. As for *Ecclesiazusae*, the leading female

Fig. 7. Red-figure Loutrophoros (wedding vase here doubling as funeral vase) by the Kleophrades Painter c. 480 BC (Louvre). Detail shows prothesis (laying-out) of dead young man, attended by four women (including his wife?), women as usual playing the leading role in death ritual.

character's claim (580-5) that she had introduced a plot new to comedy seems also to be justified.

It is not just the prominence of these women of Aristophanes, therefore, that demands our attention but also the novelty of their prominence. This was my chief reason for dealing separately with *Thesmophoriazusae*, another 'women' play in a sense but more traditional and less focussed on 'the woman question' (chapter 2). However, before we look more closely at the fictive women of *Lysistrata* and *Ecclesiazusae*, it is necessary to set them within the real-life contexts of all Athenian women, in so far as they can be adequately grasped.

*'Wives we have to be faithful guardians of the household goods and for the procreation of legitimate children' (*Demosthenes*)*

Athenian females remained, legally speaking, minors throughout their lives and did not therefore strictly count as citizens but as daughters, wives, etc. of (male) citizens. These disabilities were politically crippling: they had no vote, they could not represent themselves in court. But they were not without all compensation. Religion was essentially political in Classical Athens, as we have seen (esp. chapter 1), and in religion women were in some respects equal partners in rights and duties, in others uniquely privileged both collectively and individually. This duality and ambiguity of women's formal, public status are crucial to our understanding of their social position.

Ambivalence also surrounds their place in the household and home, although here the situation is further complicated by economics. The wife of a rich man had quite simply far more 'household goods' to be the 'faithful guardian' of than did the wife of a poor man, which increased her potential status but at the same time heightened the husband's anxiety over her performance of her indispensable economic function as household manager (note that 'economic' derives from the Greek for 'household', *oikos*). It also intensified his desire to cocoon her from external male intrusion, particularly adultery, since that would not only compromise his standing in the eyes of his male peers (the cuckold is a perennial figure of ribald jest in Mediterranean masculine society) but might also be detrimental to his economic status if it resulted in the birth of unwanted children with a claim on the patrimony.

Fear of wifely adultery was exacerbated by what seems to have been the universal ancient Greek masculine perception that women derived far more satisfaction from sexual intercourse than men – precisely nine times more, according to the legendary Teiresias who had experience on both sides of the blanket! The wives of poor men, though, were not quite so jealously or zealously protected, partly because their husbands had less materially to lose, but mainly because, to add to their routine domestic chores of food-preparation and clothesmaking, it might be necessary for the household's sheer survival to send the wife out to sell flowers or ribbons in the market, perhaps, or wet-nurse the children of economically better-off but milk-poor women.

On the other hand, both rich and poor Athenian wives had one inestimable quality in common: thanks to Pericles' citizenship law of 451 only they could produce legitimate male children, sons who might one day both assume control of their own households and become full Athenian citizens. This was the point of the formula that accompanied the formal betrothal (*enguē*) of an Athenian girl (who, like Demosthenes' sister, might be as young as five at the time of betrothal and would be married at puberty to guarantee her virginity). 'I give you this virgin', said her father or other male guardian (*kurios*, literally 'lord and master') to the future bridegroom or his *kurios*, 'for the ploughing of legitimate offspring' – an earthy metaphor well understood in this essentially agricultural society. In this absolutely fundamental respect an Athenian wife, that is the daughter of a legally wedded Athenian father and Athenian mother, was in an indefeasibly superior position to all other females in Athens and Attica, whether free or slave. Feminine sexual competition she regularly had to endure, from the slave girls of the household or up-market prostitutes called coyly 'companions' (*hetairai*) in the case of a richer husband, or from common prostitutes (*pornai*, whence our 'pornography') of the Kerameikos and Peiraeus red-light districts if the husband was poorer. But she and she alone could enable her husband to continue his name and perpetuate the citizen body of Athens.

This basic equality of legitimising and reproductive function common to all married Athenian women (and almost all women did get married: *gunē* meant 'wife' as well as 'woman') was naturally expressed ritually – and with all the usual ambivalence – in the field of religion. Polluted and polluting though they were thought to be by menstruation and childbirth, yet their role in private family burial and civic sacrificial ritual alike was considered utterly indispensable.

Quite literally vital, that is lifegiving, was their participation in religious rituals basically concerned with the fertility of plants, animals and especially of course humans, most conspicuously in the women-only festivals of the earth-mother goddesses Demeter and her daughter Persephone.

This is where we return to Aristophanes. For it was at the Thesmophoria festival, as we saw in chapter 2, that the women plotted to do away with Euripides in *Thesmophoriazusae*; and it was at the Skira festival that the women of *Ecclesiazusae* originally carried the proposals for a *gunaikokratia* ('Feminocracy') to replace the existing male-dominated *dēmokratia* – proposals that were later passed surreptitiously and illegally at a packed meeting of the ostensibly men-only citizen Assembly. But more even than in those two plays, it is in *Lysistrata* that Aristophanes exploits for comic effect the licensed, irreplaceable and public participation of women in Athenian civic religion.

Public spaces and private lives

The Acropolis was an exclusively sacred space. Always physically in the background during a theatrical performance (chapter 2), it could also be deliberately brought to the foreground of the audience's consciousness by a typically Aristophanic *coup de théâtre*. For the Acropolis was the one civic space where it was entirely natural and unremarkable for large numbers of Athenian citizen women to be collectively active and at the same time visible to unrelated men; and it was from here that the sexually ambiguous Athena, a perpetual virgin born from the head of her father, exercised her patronal sway over Athens in various guises (esp. Polias 'City-Protecting', Parthenos 'Virgin', and Nike 'Victory'), ministered to by her several priestesses. What could be more 'natural' therefore than for the women of Athens, in pursuit of their aim of bringing the Peloponnesian War to a speedy end, to seize and occupy the Acropolis, and to do so under the command of one Lysistrata ('Dissolver of Armies') whose name is a straight 'translation' of that of the real priestess of Athena Polias, Lysimakhe? What, on the other hand, could be more *un*natural than this feminine intrusion into the exclusively masculine spheres of war- and peace-making? It is precisely in that sort of juxtaposition of the plausibly ordinary with the fantastically abnormal that the root of *Lysistrata*'s humour lies.

The Acropolis occupation, however, was but the outward and

visible sign of a private and domestic revolt no less at variance with traditional masculine prerogatives. *Lysistrata* opens with a secret international delegate conference of Greek women convened by Lysistrata. With considerable difficulty she persuades her sisters to leave unsatisfied the craving for sex that their gender was supposed to suffer from and embark on a sex-strike, in order to force their war-mongering husbands to the peace-negotiating table. This decision was quadruply or even quintuply fantastic.

Real Greek married women from different states almost never had occasion to meet, even in peacetime. In 411, when the territory of Attica was permanently occupied by a Spartan garrison, such a secret gathering of the international mothers' union was unthinkable. We know virtually nothing about the normal practical arrangement of sexual relations between Greek husbands and wives within the privacy of their homes; but, given the free, legal and conventionally acceptable availability of both homosexual and heterosexual sex outside marriage for Greek men, it would be odd if they did not also expect to hold and typically take the initiative in intramarital sexual relations. Thus for wives to decide to withhold sex indefinitely from their husbands within the home (as distinct from the regular and temporary ritual abstinence practised in fertility festivals like the Thesmophoria) was the world turned upside down.

Nor was it an obviously logical move. Their husbands were after all 'at the front': how could the wives deny the men something they were not anyway in a position to give them? But finally, and most damagingly of all, there was no good, pragmatic reason for the wives to suppose that *their* denial of sexual gratification to their husbands would inevitably achieve the desired end of global peace. Only in the world of comic fantasy, where by convention anything not actually mentioned in a play was deemed not to exist, could Aristophanes' female protagonists have conveniently 'forgotten' the availability to the husbands of a wide variety of extra-marital sexual outlets (messmates, boys, slaves, prostitutes etc.), even if it were true – as it may have been – that successful marital sexual relations were normally rated superior to all other kinds by most members of both sexes.

Granted, then, that the 'plot' of *Lysistrata* depends for its success on a prodigious suspension of disbelief on the part of the audience, was Aristophanes concerned to play the ensuing (literal as well as metaphorical) battle of the sexes solely for the laughs? That is certainly what is suggested by such scenes as the prick-teasing by

Myrrhine (in real life the name of a priestess of Athena Nike, but useful to Aristophanes primarily because *myrrhinē*, 'myrtle-wreath', was also used to refer to the female sex organ) of her husband Kinesias (allocated to the Attic deme Paiania to justify the punning Kinesias Paionides or 'Roger Screw-ton of Bang-cock'), or the unbearably priapic reaction of both Spartan and Athenian men when Lysistrata presents to them Reconciliation (*Diallagē*) personified as the literal ancient equivalent of a modern 'sex-goddess' like Marilyn Monroe.

Fig. 8. Attic red-figure vase by the Flying Angel Painter, c. 500-475 BC. Young woman carrying phallus-bird uncovers basket of dildoes: female Athenian reality or male Athenian fantasy?

On the other hand, many modern scholars are unwilling to accept that Aristophanes had no personal stake in the advocacy (however unrealistic) of peace and panhellenic coexistence, a theme already given conspicuous airings in *Acharnians* and of course *Peace* (see chapter 6). And they point to the unusual consistency with which (so they claim) the character of the eponymous heroine is drawn, and to the apparent gravity of the lengthy *agōn*-speeches of hers which substitute in this play for a choral *parabasis*, as evidence for their view that Aristophanes was criticising the artificiality and harmful effects of traditional Greek male values. To put this important difference of opinion into proper perspective we must enlarge our vision to embrace the other surviving play of female intrusion.

Gynecocracy rules – or is it a knockabout?

Almost twenty years after the performance of *Lysistrata* the fortunes of Athens were beginning to revive after the cataclysmic experience of defeat by Sparta in the Peloponnesian War. But she was again involved in a major war, this time reliant on resources not her own, and could hardly be said to have recovered from the previous conflict. This was the setting for a yet more daring Aristophanic experiment – or extravaganza – in female intrusion upon male space: the establishment of a *gunaikokratia* at Athens under the aegis of another Athenian woman with a symbolically suitable and punning name, Praxagora ('She who gets things done in the agora' – meaning both 'civic centre' and 'market'). But Praxagora or rather Aristophanes was not satisfied with the mere establishment of a gynecocracy (something possibly anticipated on the Athenian comic stage, and certainly in multi-media myths of Amazonia). This was to be an 'ideal state' run economically speaking on communalistic lines and sexually speaking on the basis of positive discrimination in favour of old and ugly women – in other words, a far more drastic inversion of everyday Athenian realities than had been contemplated, let alone effected, in *Lysistrata*.

Yet although there is a marked difference here between the two plays, it is a difference of degree, not kind. In both, the basic comic idea is the confusion of the private world of the household with the public world of the state by means of the reversal of the 'natural' balance of initiative and power between the sexes. Thus the women of *Ecclesiazusae*, once they have effected their *coup* and won control of the state by exploiting its legal machinery (as had the real-life oligarchic counter-revolutionaries of 411), in the first place treat the *polis* of Athens as though it were an outsize *oikos* ('household'), reducing what Greek theorists called *politikē* (the art of politics, or state-government) to *oikonomia* (household management). Secondly, they extend the notion of female sexual initiative to the point of grotesque caricature by translating it into public political terms and passing a law compelling men to have sex with any woman who demands it, in strict order of age and ugliness where two or more women compete for the sexual favours of the same man.

Much time and effort have been wasted over the years in trying to determine whether or not Aristophanes' women rulers were conceived independently of the women Guardians in Plato's *Republic* and, if not, who influenced whom. But even if it were possible to reach a consensus, that debate overlooks or bypasses the most important question about the former, which is why Aristophanes thought his audience would or should have found Praxagora & Co. funny. True, there was much humour to be derived from theatrical transvestism and the satirising of male sexual and economic foibles. But even the most fervent proponents of a purely comic and festive Aristophanes have felt uncomfortable with the long drawn-out penultimate scene of haggling in *Ecclesiazusae*, in which three progressively more repellent old women wrangle over a luscious young man whose mind and other portions of his anatomy are set on a fourth, much younger and presumably adulterous housewife. Rather than resort to various lame and unconvincing expedients to explain away this scene of horror (e.g. the waning of Aristophanes' dramatic powers, a decline not otherwise much in evidence), attention is better focused on the informing theme of the play as a whole, which is identical to that of *Frogs*: how best can the state be saved?

Aristophanes as sexual politician

Under the influence of the Sophistic 'wisdom' to which Aristophanes had taken great exception (chapter 3), all existing conventions (*nomoi*) of behaviour and belief at Athens had been subjected to relentless scrutiny on and off the stage, not excluding intercourse between the sexes inside and outside the domestic domain, and the relationship of the private household to the public commonwealth. In the circumstances of c. 392 it was perhaps especially difficult to maintain like Voltaire's Dr Pangloss that all was for the best in the best of all possible worlds – or at least to rule out of court 'a certain feminism' both within the home and in the affairs of state. Yet that, I believe, is what Aristophanes sought to do.

For even if it was part of all comedy's social and ritual function to reaffirm the society's traditional norms, the spirit in which he savages the notions of economic communalism and female sexual and political emancipation in *Ecclesiazusae* seems to me radically unlike the much gentler if no less disillusioned send-up of male as well as female sexuality in *Lysistrata* – where in any case the female intrusion had not ultimately threatened the radical demarcation of male and female roles in the public political arena. So whatever we may think of Aristophanes' alleged pacifism or panhellenism in that play, we should not hesitate to infer that in *Ecclesiazusae* he was playing the dangerously serious game of sexual politics – and battling on the side of conservative masculinism rather than in the interests of constructive social criticism.

Chapter 5
The Politics of Aristophanes

The great modern debate

I begin with two facts of near-contemporary British life:

Fact 1: in January 1987 the two writers of the television comedy series 'Yes, Minister' and 'Yes, Prime Minister' were presented with an award by the pressure-group Campaign for Freedom of Information (CFI) for what the citation hailed as their 'unrivalled and witty exposure of the cynicism of Whitehall secrecy'.

Fact 2: 'Yes, Prime Minister' was then on record as being the favourite viewing of one Margaret Thatcher, MP and PM – or, as a certain poet might have said, of our very own jag-toothed Leaderene.

In light of the many controversial political issues where freedom of information has not obviously been the overriding priority of Mrs Thatcher's governments, I find these two facts just a trifle incongruous, their juxtaposition verging even on the absurd. But they do nevertheless neatly raise in brief compass the two main interpretative problems that any reading of Aristophanes' politics must inescapably confront:

(1) A public political pressure-group of the utmost sincerity and gravity can today treat a piece of dramatised comic fiction as a serious expression of an unambiguous political message – is this *the* or even *a* right way to read the two plays selected for special attention in this chapter, *Knights* and *Wasps* (selected because key aspects of the Athenian democratic process are placed at the centre of the comedy)?

(2) The same present-day comic drama series can be viewed, not just without misgivings but with professed positive pleasure, by a politician whose policy and programme do not exactly coincide with those of the CFI – can these two plays of Aristophanes, too, legitimately or justifiably be read in such contradictory ways, opposite as regards both intention and effect?

43

Comic politics or the politics of comedy?

I argued in chapter 3 that Aristophanes did mean to be taken seriously as a traditional didactic poet, even if his peculiar dramatic genius and the theatrical-religious context within which he exercised it dictated that the seriousness be masked by a variety of comic devices. There is reliable ancient support from the political sphere for this way of taking Aristophanes.

Historically, what Aristotle called the 'iambic form', that is personal invective delivered originally in iambic metre, was a much older literary art-form than comedy in its dramatic, Athenian dress. Its originator, or at least the man credited with its invention, was Arkhilokhos of Paros and Thasos, a roistering aristocrat who flourished around the middle of the seventh century BC. A noted follower about a century later was the scatological Hipponax of Ephesos, but it was not before about 450 that Krates incorporated such iambs within the framework of a recognisably dramatic comic plot, where they were exempted from the scope of Athenian prohibitions on slander by the licensed freedom of speech (*parrhēsia*) of a religious festival.

However, in 440/39 for some reason (perhaps connected with the current revolt of Samos?) and again in about 415/4 (when the reason was surely to do with the sacrilegious scandals of herm-smashing and profanation of the Eleusinian Mysteries) that licence was suspended or restricted by specific measures of the Athenian Assembly. Moreover, according to a probably youthful and Sophist-trained oligarch pamphleteering somewhere around 425, the *dēmos* did not allow itself to be insulted in comedy, although it permitted the abuse of individuals, generally rich, well-born and powerful. The first part of that assertion cannot be literally true, or it is true only up to a point (see discussion of the character Demos in *Knights,* below). But the assertion as a whole does suggest that by various means the *dēmos* which wielded the power in the state kept a watching brief over the ways in which the comic poets used their licensed privilege of political invective.

It was therefore from his own point of view entirely natural and indeed obligatory for a would-be 'champion' of the *dēmos* – or, as we would say, leading democratic politician – to attempt to exercise that brief on the People's behalf from time to time. Such a time arose after the Great Dionysia of 426, to Aristophanes' cost. As the poet himself, speaking through the mask of the as yet unnamed hero Dikaiopolis (a part he may have taken in person), was most anxious to inform the audience of *Acharnians* at the immediately succeeding Lenaia:

> And I know about myself, what I suffered at Kleon's hands because of last year's comedy. He dragged me into the Council chamber and began slandering me...
>
> (lines 378-80, trans. A. Sommerstein)

Later on in the play, again exploiting the ambiguity between the playwright and the now named character of Dikaiopolis, Aristophanes refers once more to his *Babylonians* ('last year's comedy'):

> And what I'll say, though startling, will be right.
> For this time Kleon can't accuse me of
> Running down the city when foreigners are here.
> We're by ourselves; it's the Lenaion contest;
> No foreigners are here yet, for the tribute
> And allies from the cities have not come.
>
> (lines 501-5, trans. D.M. MacDowell)

Kleon, that is to say, had taken *Babylonians* seriously, or – if this was merely a pretext for getting at a fellow-demesman with whom he had a bitter personal feud (cf. A Brief 'Life') – had seen nothing odd about using it as a ground for impeaching its author before the democracy's chief organ of day-to-day administration, the Council of 500.

The fact that his impeachment had failed is of course why Aristophanes brags about it, extracting the maximum humour from Kleon's discomfiture. But that fact does not mean that Kleon had been wrong in principle to take a comedy seriously, only that he had failed to convince the relevant Councillors to share his view of the damage allegedly done to Athens by this particular play. Aristophanes, we may suspect, had in his usual manner innovated in such a way as to stretch the hitherto accepted limits of comic licence. Kleon, on the other hand, in his role of 'defender of the faith' or the wisdom of the ancestors (the role we see him portrayed in by Thucydides, but not, significantly, Aristophanes), had felt obliged to resist the innovation, motivated partly by personal enmity but more especially by the desire to propagate his gospel of how Athens should rule her subject-allies of the Athenian Empire (apparently the main issue at stake in the *Babylonians*).

Aristophanes, my Aristophanes

Even comedy, then, could be taken seriously by the Athenians and should be taken seriously by us. But in what sense did it 'know what is right' (*Acharnians* 500)? How precisely should we read any political messages we may detect in *Knights* and *Wasps*? In my view, argued in this chapter, he used populist comedy to discredit the political system, deceiving the *dēmos* like the politicians he fantastically portrayed. My Aristophanes, in other words, is an orator in comic (dis)guise, employing many of the same rhetorical techniques practised in Assembly or lawcourts by the real-life politicians whom he satirises or flays in order to persuade his audience towards a new and in his opinion improved understanding of democratic politics.

On the other hand, since Aristophanes undoubtedly also burned to win the first prize, and to do that required making most of the audience laugh most of the time and go away happy, he could not afford blatantly and unambiguously to attack the democratic system as such (as, say, Thucydides, Plato and the anonymous pamphleteer could). Nor could he afford to give most of the audience the impression that he did not share and endorse their fundamental commitment to radical democracy. His message, in short, *had* to be pretty heavily wrapped up in comic trappings, which would inevitably hide its anti-democratic source from all but the sharpest playgoers. Thus the best or rather the only way open to Aristophanes to achieve what I take to be his political ends was to appear to take the side of the masses, the *dēmos*, or at any rate a section of them (a point to which I shall return in the next chapter), and either defend them from those whom they mistakenly believed to be their friends (allegedly corrupt politicians like Kleon above all) or expose to them the moral and political errors of supposedly typical democratic citizens (such as jurors like Philokleon in *Wasps*).

'Once a knight's enough'?

The chief target of *Knights* is unambiguously Kleon, here punningly parodied as the blustering (*paphlazōn*) Paphlagonian slave of old 'Demos Pyknites' (Demos of Pnyx Hill). By a bold stroke, which carried the risk of diluting the audience's empathy with the vicious satire, Aristophanes used as his Chorus representatives of the socially élite Knights (*hippeis*), perhaps the top five per cent of the citizen body in economic terms. He did this partly because in reality Kleon did identify politically with the hoplites (heavy-armed infantrymen who could afford to supply their own equipment and own a slave to look after it) and especially the sailors (the poorest group, paid from state funds) against the cavalry (to which probably both he and Aristophanes were financially qualified to belong). But he did so also because this enabled him dramatically to heighten the contrast he wished to draw between the 'good' (*agathoi*), i.e. well-born and morally admirable, Knights and the vulgar guttersnipe of a tanner that he makes Kleon/Paphlagon out to be.

But in order to avert the risk of audience-alienation (arising from the fact that cavalrymen in reality would usually not hold radically democratic opinions), Aristophanes was careful both to credit the Knights with enlightened views of the military and political role of their social inferiors (e.g. in the first *parabasis*) and to debit them with some of those features of dress and behaviour that in actual fact made them widely objectionable to the masses (579). And he was equally scrupulous to call them just *agathoi* (225) and not, as they surely called themselves in reality, *kaloikagathoi*, 'beautiful and good', since he was reserving the noble epithet *kalos* for the transformed Demos whose epiphany constitutes the play's climax.

To allegorise the *dēmos* of Athens as an old man was not peculiarly Aristophanic. Precisely the same representation, though visual rather than verbal, was employed in the carved relief that stands at the head of an inscribed law against tyranny passed in 337/6. Fear of tyranny, which Aristophanes duly exploits by associating it with Kleon (e.g. 447-9), was a perennial concern of the democracy, indeed part of its foundation or charter myth of the Tyrannicides (Harmodios and Aristogeiton: see *Athens under the Tyrants*, by J.A. Smith, also in this series). To choose an elderly man to stand for the citizenry and state of democratic Athens was a way of celebrating the virtue of political wisdom that came with age, experience and adherence to traditional values. It corresponded to the constitutional facts that, although an Athenian might vote in the Assembly or during an ostracism from the age of 20, he might not become a Councillor, juror or official before he was 30, by when he would normally have become the head of a household and a father, with all the powers and responsibilities those positions implied.

However, some old men, so far from being wise elder statesmen, were notoriously senile and irrationally obstinate, and proverbially there's no fool like an old fool. The personified Demos of Aristophanes (himself still a very young man in 424) embodies both of these popular stereotypes, in succession. Indeed, it is precisely the transformation of Demos from mercilessly exploited, bad-tempered old fool to disabused and perky citizen of the good old school that constitutes the play's dominant plot-device.

Fig. 9. Relief adorning stele recording Athenian law against t ⁀anny, 337/6 BC. *The goddess Demokratia crowns Demos (People of Athens).*

The character doing the merciless exploiting of Demos at the start of *Knights* is of course Paphlagon/Kleon, shown as a 'loud-mouthed upstart divisive coercive tanner demagogue' (in one recent scholar's splendid phrase). Since at least 427 and probably ever since the death of Pericles in 429, the real Kleon, who was wealthy (perhaps from the proceeds of a slave-tannery rather than landowning) but not an aristocrat like Pericles, had been the single most influential Athenian politician. Technically an 'orator', ideologically a 'champion' of the People, his political function was to act as a *dēmagōgos*.

This meant literally 'leader of the *dēmos*', but in the backbiting atmosphere of Athenian high politics it was a short step from the etymological meaning to the pejorative connotations of *mis*leader of the People and rabble-rouser – the very connotations of our own 'demagogue'. It was of course in this sense that Aristophanes allegorically presented Kleon as one of old Demos' slaves: the most recently bought but already the most influential.

What was to be done? With comic 'logic' two other slaves of Demos' household decide to fight fire with fire, by finding someone who will out-demagogue the arch-demagogue or – in Aristophanes' familiar marketplace metaphor – outsell the tanner's leather goods with some yet more vulgar and demotic commodity. A divinely-foretold Sausage-Seller, born and bred in the nether reaches of the agora, fits the bill to perfection, his faltering courage buoyed up by Knightly encouragement. The *agōn* between these rival suitors of Demos simultaneously satirizes homosexual courtship, the current extravagant language of political discourse, and most importantly what Thucydides later identified as a key factor in the post-Periclean decline and eventual defeat of Athens: namely that, whereas Pericles had led the *dēmos* and told it what it should do, his successors like Kleon were on the contrary led by the *dēmos* in the sense that they fell over themselves in their flattery of the masses (cf. Eupolis fr. 117 on the decline of leadership quality). This is only one of the revealing coincidences between Thucydides' retrospective historical evaluation and Aristophanes' contemporary comic representation of Kleon and the demagogues.

However, in the upside-down world of comedy the Paphlagonian gets and must get his come-uppance at the hands – or rather the consistently raucous voice – of the Sausage-Seller, both in the Council (offstage) and in front of old Demos (standing for the Assembly). The latter victory is effected in three stages, the last being a practical demonstration of the leitmotif of all Aristophanic abuse of politicians, that the Paphlagonian had consistently been ripping off his master by keeping for himself the lion's share of his illicit super-profits. Amid paratragic lamentation at his foreordained fate the Paphlagonian slave is forced to exchange roles with the Sausage-Seller in a typically comic inversion. But he is also literally marginalised, condemned to sell his wares as far away as possible from the political centre of the city.

This is the signal for Demos to become *kalos* (1321), or rather to become beautiful *again*, as he had been in the 'good old days' before most of the audience (with whom Demos is now explicitly identified) were born. Praise of the 'good old days' and this climactic flattery of the audience proved a winning combination. *They* at least were not Kleon's dupes; and such a dramatic trouncing, the comic equivalent of the audit (*euthunai*) that all office-holders had to undergo from the Council and sometimes the People's jurycourts, would remind Kleon symbolically where the real power in the state lay. So they gave Aristophanes the first prize – and quite consistently elected Kleon as one of the ten Generals for 424/3 shortly afterwards (see *Clouds* 581-94). But the select few *sōphrones* ('knowledgeably prudent') among them, who according to Thucydides had previously looked forward to Kleon's coming a cropper as stand-in General for the Pylos campaign of 425 (referred to ten times in *Knights*), presumably just groaned at the congenital fickleness and gullibility of the ignorant mob.

Courtroom drama or kicking the ass of the law

In its *dénouement* and happy ultimate transformation of one of its two main characters, *Wasps* bears an uncanny resemblance to *Knights*. Only the resemblance is not in fact uncanny. *Knights* had been a success, *Clouds* at the 423 Dionysia a flop. So *Wasps*, which Aristophanes staged at the Lenaia of 422, was designed to be a continuation of *Knights* by other means, a repeat of that successful basic formula. In the event, it was placed second, but not, surely, because of its plot-structure.

Courtroom dramas often make good theatre, thanks to the built-in dramatic element in a formal legal trial. But in democratic Athens the theatre itself could become a courtroom, literally as well as metaphorically. Thus in *Wasps* Aristophanes cleverly exploits this by staging a farcical *agōn* (trial) within a play about real trials (*dikai*, *agōnes*) in the popular jurycourts (*dikastēria*) that was itself part of a theatrical contest (*agōn*) watched and adjudicated by an Athenian audience, most of whom were or had been or would be real-world jurors (*dikastai*).

It was a group of supposedly typical citizen jurors, elderly, venomous, and mercenary, who formed the eponymous Chorus of *Wasps*. But this was not the first nor the last Aristophanic comedy to satirise jurymen (the plot of *Birds*, for instance, 'takes off' from their poisonous existence: see next chapter), and always in exactly the same terms, stressing their age, vindictiveness and greed for pay.

In political reality every year 6000 citizens in good standing aged 30 or above were empanelled by lot to staff at need, also by lot, and for a modest fee (three obols a day, recently raised from two on Kleon's proposal) the various courts which sat on between 150 and 200 days per annum. The use of the lot was considered peculiarly democratic, as was the very idea of state pay, which maximised the pool of potential jurors and so the chances for as many citizens as possible to do their civic duty. For being a juryman was a public, political act, essential to the conception and functioning of the Athenian direct democracy, in which the same citizens legislated and sat in judgment (they were judges as well as jurors in our sense) on the legality both of individual behaviour and of the state's laws and decrees. Aristophanes, therefore, in selecting jurors for his Chorus, was not picking on some marginal social group (as the Knights were), but on a thoroughly representative element among the poorer sections of the active citizenry, some of whom took their job so deadly seriously that they carried their juror's identity-token with them into the grave.

Fig. 10. Jurors' ballots, bronze, 4th century BC, from Agora of Athens. Inscribed 'civic ballot', those with pierced axles were for 'guilty', solid for 'not guilty'.

In *Lysistrata*, too, Aristophanes uses a Chorus (strictly, a semi-chorus) of old men, and, however unseriously the project of peacemaking may have been intended, it is pretty clear that in the end the audience were supposed to sympathise with them in so far as they were won round to the peace that enabled a resumption of 'normal' life. Similarly, if more ambiguously, the Chorus of *Wasps* is revealed ultimately in a sympathetic light. For it is portrayed as won round to the unorthodox views of the character whom Aristophanes uses to guide the play's action – another recalcitrant son, like Pheidippides in *Clouds*.

The plot, in brief, calls for the conversion of one of the Chorus' friends, a fanatical professional juror called Philokleon or 'Love-Kleon', from his overmastering mania for jury-service to what Aristophanes represents as less publicly harmful – though no more intrinsically virtuous – high living. The chosen instrument of his conversion is his son Bdelykleon or 'Loathe-Kleon'.

In over half of the extant plays jurors and jury-service are censured on the grounds that jurors are in it mainly for the money, secondarily to gratify their private lusty vindictiveness, and not at all out of a sense of civic duty or pride. But in *Wasps* this theme of vilification reaches a crescendo, diminished somewhat only by the pantomime antics of the buffoonish Philokleon. Even some of those modern interpreters who in general are anxious to deny that Aristophanes used his plays as political vehicles concede that such harping on a motif in a consistent way may betray the playwright's own view of a topic. When this is combined, as here, with a continuation of his abuse of Kleon (which we have found reason to believe was neither just traditional comic invective nor an expression of purely personal animosity), the strong suspicion arises that Aristophanes' hostility was not directed only at particular jurors or abuses, but at the very democratic jury-system as such. Can it be merely coincidence that the dramatically inorganic and straightforwardly serious plea for an amnesty advanced in the *parabasis* of *Frogs* (686-705) concerns the very same extreme oligarchs who in 411 had briefly succeeded in abolishing the democratic system of popular jurisdiction?

It has been objected to this line of interpretation that nowhere in *Wasps* or any other play does Aristophanes give vent to the view actually held by non-radical democrats or oligarchs that Athens should revert constitutionally to the 'good old days' before 462/1, when elected officials acted as judges, and jurors, who sat solely as a court of appeal and not also of first instance, were unpaid. But even to hint at that view would of course have been theatrical suicide – the kind of thing Euripides might have tried in a tragedy, perhaps; but he too often paid the penalty of dramatic defeat for his bold airing of deeply unfashionable ideas to serve the prize-hungry Aristophanes as a model and guide.

The other main objection raised is that, if Aristophanes was so deeply hostile to the jury-system on principle, why did he write the part of Philokleon as he did – a lovable rogue, full of knavish tricks and remarkably versatile, with life pulsing in the old dog yet? Again, that seems to me no objection whatsoever. On the contrary, it was a shrewd dramatic move of the (so I believe) politically reactionary, not merely 'moderate' Aristophanes to paint the man whose ideology and way of life are pilloried for most of the play until he is re-educated by his son as not indelibly and incurably wicked but misguided and misled – by none other than Philokleon's original idol and Bdelykleon's (and Aristophanes') *bête noire*, the real live Kleon.

However, even the slapstick humour of Philokleon's clowning (e.g. 169-95, the mock-heroic attempt at escape under a donkey modelled on Odysseus' successful ruse against the Cyclops), the brilliant farce of the spoof trial scene in Philokleon's house (760-1008: the prosecutor, a surrogate Kleon, and the defendant are both dogs), the original idea of taking the Chorus off dancing, and the shrewd appeal to the audience's goodwill through Philokleon's eventual metamorphosis – even these were not enough to secure the first prize for Aristophanes. Perhaps (to borrow his own favourite sheep-metaphor for the misled and put-upon masses with whom he affected to identify, e.g. *Knights* 749-55, *Wasps* 31-6) the wool had not been pulled over the audience's eyes so effectively in 422 as it had been two years before?

Chapter 6
Aristophanic E(u)topias

Erewhon or the Land of Cockaigne?

When Sir Thomas More coined the word 'utopia', he was perfectly well aware as a good classical scholar that his invention was inherently ambiguous. Was it an *ou*-topia, a 'No-Place', or an *eu*-topia, a 'Place of Well-Faring'? In his own practice the answer is that it was more the former than the latter, more a peculiarly dramatic and vivid way of exposing the moral flaws in existing societal arrangements than a practicable blueprint for a new-model society. The same could well be said of the *Republic* of Plato, and quite appropriately so too, since More was deeply indebted both in conception and detail to Plato and through him to Sparta – or rather to the idealised or imaginary visions of Sparta propagated by philosophers and politicians mainly in democratic Athens for their various reactionary purposes.

One of the earliest literary exponents of the Spartan 'mirage' was the philosopher-politician Kritias, a relative of Plato and one-time pupil of Socrates who seems to have tried to translate words into deeds by heading the pro-Spartan oligarchic junta of the 'Thirty Tyrants' in 404-3. It was probably largely Socrates' connection with men like Kritias – rather than the *Clouds* (see chapter 3) – that cost him his life in 399. But however partial to oligarchy Aristophanes may have been, there is no reason for supposing that he subscribed to this Spartophile brand, and some reason (esp. *Ecclesiazusae*) for supposing that he did not, even though it has to be said that he was on the whole remarkably gentle with the state against which his own was at war for three-quarters of his adult life (see further below). And his utopias, unlike those of Kritias, were of course escapist fantasies rather than plans for action, as befitted their carnival context.

That, however, did not make them any less serious fantasies. For it is very noticeable that, with the (partial and ambiguous) exception of *Plutus* (chapter 7), we do not find in Aristophanes' extant plays the strain of comic utopianism according to which (as in Krates' *Wild Beasts*) in some utterly desirable future there will be no need for anyone to work (not even slaves, since there won't be any slaves), because all the necessities of life and many of its luxuries will be constantly and abundantly on tap. Indeed, in *Ecclesiazusae* (651) it is explicitly said that under the ideal Feminocracy slaves will do all the work.

Paradoxically, therefore, Aristophanic utopianism typically stays rather closer to the ground – paradoxically, because the three utopian comedies I shall be discussing specifically in this chapter are all structured by aerial flights of absurdist fantasy. In *Acharnians* the hero arranges for someone to fly over to Sparta to conclude a private peace-treaty on his behalf, since there is clearly no prospect of his state's making peace. In *Peace* the hero takes flight himself, but beyond the earth's atmosphere up to the celestial world of the gods of Mount Olympos on a mission to spring the goddess Peace from the cavernous clutches of the War god. Finally, in *Birds* two Athenians, fed up with their obsessively jury-minded compatriots, escape to the aethereal realm of the Birds, whom they persuade to found a city somewhere 'up there' between the spheres of mortal men and the Olympians.

'A definite plea for peace'?

So Gilbert Murray interpreted *Acharnians*, which has at any rate definitely been one of the chief battlegrounds in modern times for those who propose and those who oppose the notion of Aristophanes as some sort of propagandist as well as – or rather than – 'pure' comic dramatist. I happen to agree with Murray's interpretation, though with an important qualification (below). But even those who do not are bound to concede that peace was a major topic of conversation off the stage at Athens in 426/5 when *Acharnians* was devised and victoriously performed at the Lenaia.

The Great Peloponnesian War between Athens and Sparta and their respective allies was in its sixth year. On top of the physical damage to lives, buildings and crops inflicted by the Spartan invasions of Attica in 431, 430 and 428, the Athenians had suffered great mental anguish. Most of them were countrymen, living outside the pale of urban settlement in the city of Athens and the Peiraeus. It grieved them as well as inconvenienced them to have to leave even temporarily (no more than a couple of months at most) their rural demes, which they regarded with a sentiment something like local patriotism (the modern Italian *amor di campanile*). Overcrowding in Athens, moreover, had aggravated the effects of the Great Plague which struck first in 430 and again in 427/6 and which must have seemed like a punishment from the gods. Indeed, in 430 the Athenians in their despair had actually sacked Pericles from the Generalship and sued for peace, only to be rudely rebuffed by the gloating Spartans. Between 430 and 426/5 things had got no worse, but there were few reasons for thinking they had got much better. The real breakthrough at Pylos still lay in the future.

Aristophanes therefore knew what he was doing when he chose for his hero a disgruntled countryman and cleverly placed in opposition to him a Chorus of bellicose and vengeful farmers from Akharnai. This was one of the largest of the Attic demes, in the front line of Spartan land-invasion, and the proud possessor of the only Attic deme-cults of the war-god Ares and Athena Areia ('Warrior Athena'). The plot conforms to a widespread Aristophanic 'if-only' type of fantasy. The little man conceives a big idea to fulfil a grandiose ambition appealing to the innermost dreams of the ordinary Athenian. The means of fulfilment are inevitably abnormal and superhuman, and the necessary links in the chain of cause and effect are conveniently broken for the hero's sake. But in order to make the fantasy seem as real as possible it is initially set in an apparently normal, true-to-life context – a meeting of the Athenian Assembly.

This is not Aristophanes' only presentation of an Assembly. He has another go at one in *Ecclesiazusae*, and in *Thesmophoriazusae*, where the opening ritual prayers and curses of the real all-male citizen Assembly are suitably adapted by the women to their immediate objective of destroying Euripides. But the Assembly of *Acharnians* (1-203) is deliberately the most authentic of all, sandwiched as it is between the hero's opening soliloquy (he's arrived first on the Pnyx and can't wait for proceedings to start – 'I'm alone,/I sigh, I yawn, I stretch myself, I fart [inevitably],/I'm bored, I doodle, I pull out hairs...') and his exasperated decision to commission one Amphitheos to fly Hermes-like to Sparta to negotiate a private peace on his behalf. The introduction of a Persian or pseudo-Persian ambassador (great opportunity for Aristophanes' line in pidgin Greek; cf. the Scythian policeman of *Thesmophoriazusae*: chapter 2) and an army of Thracian mercenaries sustains the illusion of realism, which is neatly rounded off by the hero's claiming to feel a drop of rain – in real life a possible reason for suspending an Assembly and a considerable likelihood at the time of year when the Lenaia was held. On Amphitheos' return with 'samples' of different peace-treaties, the hero opts for the

'Thirty-Years' variety because that of course was the kind that had been broken in 431 (by Athens, in his view – see below).

The following scene leads into the *agōn* between Chorus and hero but its importance for our present purposes is wider than that. For it encapsulates the peculiar mix that constitutes Aristophanic eutopianism: City (in the sense of the *polis* of the Athenians, not the urban 'downtown' areas), countryside, peace, and festival (especially rural and Dionysiac) with its abnormal abundance of food, drink, song and sex. Thus the first and 'obvious' thing the hero tries to do when he has made his private peace is celebrate the Rural Dionysia festival in his deme of Kholleidai.

Later on in the play, after the hero's name has been revealed as Dikaiopolis ('Just City' or 'He who sets the city to rights') and the Chorus have been won round with the aid of some cheerful burlesque of Euripides to his ideal of peace, it is time for the Anthesteria festival, celebrated actually in the month after the Lenaia. So while the Chorus' now abandoned champion Lamakhos (a real Athenian, but his name, 'Extremely Warlike', lent itself to the parody of him as a swashbuckling soldierly swaggart) is on guard deep amid the winter snow on Parnes, Dikaiopolis is living the life of Riley, feasting with a priest of Dionysos. To ram the point home, as it were, the play ends with Dikaiopolis repeating the phallic by-play of the Rural Dionysia scene and lurching drunkenly and triumphantly off to bed, his comic phallos rampant, a young girl on each arm.

Just how serious was any or all of this meant to be? Most attention, naturally enough, has been given to the lines in which Dikaiopolis, recently revealed as being so named about half an hour into the play, speaks in the autobiographical first person on behalf of the playwright (499; cf. 377-82) – uniquely so, since in other plays this is the role of the Chorus or Chorus-leader. Of course he is dressed in rags (borrowed from the eponymous hero of Euripides' *Telephus*) and curiously well versed in Euripides for an unlettered peasant; and of course his account of the 'origins of the Peloponnesian War' does not exactly coincide with any that you'll find in a modern history-book (though amusingly enough you would find it in an *ancient* one, that written by Ephoros in the fourth century BC). But were not these visual and verbal distractions intended to mask or rather to soften Aristophanes/Dikaiopolis' unpalatable message?

It has rightly been pointed out that a plea for tolerance towards, say, Hitler's Germany uttered on the London stage in 1940 is totally unthinkable – Bud Flanagan's comedy, for example, took a quite different form. But that in effect is what Aristophanes/Dikaiopolis uttered at the Lenaia of 425, prefaced it is true by 'Now I hate the Spartans intensely...' (though he doesn't feel hatred on principle, only because they've destroyed *his* vines too), but followed almost immediately by 'why do we blame it all on the Spartans?' When we find that plea for tolerance combined with abuse of 'sycophants' ('vexatious' prosecutors in the popular jurycourts) and of Kleon, and when we consider how extraordinarily mild his satire of Sparta and things Spartan typically is, then – in light of the conclusions of chapter 5 – all our worst suspicions should surely be aroused. The line that this is drama and carnival drama at that begins to wear pretty thin. What Aristophanes is advocating, I suggest, is not just peace for its own sake, but a peace from which Sparta mainly would profit. That for Aristophanes is 'what is right' (*Acharnians* 645, cf. 500).

A pacific fantasia

Aristophanes' *Peace*, staged at the Dionysia of 421 and placed second, is linked to the historical situation in which it was created more directly and obviously than any other extant play. Less than a fortnight after it was performed peace with Sparta, the so-called Peace of Nikias, was actually concluded, although negotiations had been going on since the previous summer and the terms to some extent replicated those of the armistice of 423. But precisely because of that chronological coincidence and historical connection, there was no mileage – either practical or purely dramatic – to be gained out of *advocating* peace, as there was in *Acharnians* and again in *Lysistrata* (chapter 4). So whereas the flight of fantasy in *Acharnians* was firmly grounded in authentic political practicality, in *Peace* the mood and setting are timeless and fantastic throughout.

Thus the play begins with references not to any ordinary dung-beetle (*kantharos*, the scarab-beetle of Egypt, where it was actually worshipped) but to a truly monstrous specimen for which the hero's two slaves are obliged to knead prodigiously vast cakes of its specialised fodder. And the hero, Trygaios (whose name, like *trugōidia* (*Acharnians* 500), puns on *trugē*, 'vintage'), is first presented as mad – not in the way that Philokleon the year before was mad for jury-service, nor mad 'like you' (the audience), but mad 'in an entirely brand-new way' (55). He wants to do nothing less than release the 'vineyard-lovingest of all' (308) goddess Eirene (Peace) from the cave in which she is being held captive by Polemos (War). This fantastic project required as props both the aforementioned dung-beetle (the source of much excremental humour) and the theatrical crane (*mēkhanē*, yet another dig at Euripides, this time for his *Bellerophon*).

Of course, it goes without saying, he does carry out his mission seemingly impossible, with a little help from all the 'men of Greece' (292-8) – farmers (given pride of place), sea-traders, craftsmen and foreigners, who just happen to be on hand – and after a little cajoling of the initially obstructive Hermes. And the consequences of his achievement, which are worked out in the remainder of the play, culminating in a joyous wedding celebration, are shown to be unambiguously and universally a Good Thing. So Trygaios was not, after all, mad – quite unlike Philokleon in *Wasps*, whose juromania has to be cured before the play achieves a satisfactory conclusion, whereas Trygaios remains, like Thucydides' Pericles, 'the same as I have always been'.

There is no doubt, then, that Aristophanes is lending his comic weight to the peace with Sparta that was actually about to come on stream. But was that all there was to the play? It seems to me that Aristophanes was not simply singing a pacifist hymn, but advocating a particular sort of peace and with a particular object in view.

Aristophanes himself came from an urban deme, and even though Athens in 421 BC was not the concrete jungle that Athens is in AD 1990 there was still a perceptible contrast between life in Kydathenaion and life in Athmonon, Trygaios' deme, chosen for its association with viticulture.The point of view adopted consistently in Aristophanes' comedies of escape or reconstruction is that of the above-averagely prosperous peasant farmer, someone who could not afford not to work for a living (as the 'rich' by definition could) but yet sufficiently well off to own a slave or two. In *Peace* not only the vintner-hero but the Chorus are just this sort of peasant farmers; and when the Chorus hail Trygaios as 'useful' or 'worthy' for the citizens of Athens (910-11) and as the 'saviour' of all mankind (914-15), they are by implication celebrating the salvationist quality of agriculture, especially viticulture. Trygaios' hardly modest reply that he has 'freed the mass of ordinary farmer-folk from terrible hardships' (920-1) makes plain whom he – and by extension Aristophanes – regards as the truly deserving beneficiaries of (the) peace.

Aristophanes also wrote a *Farmers* (*Geōrgoi*) and indeed a second *Peace*, apparently, in which the goddess of the first play, who had been represented as a statue, was replaced by the speaking part of 'Agriculture' personified, the 'faithful nurse, housekeeper, fellow-worker, steward, daughter and sister of Peace' (fr. 294). However, although Eirene is purely statuesque in *Peace*, she none the less dominates the second half of the play both by her physical presence and by her symbolic meanings and associations. It is these religious implications of peace which I believe Aristophanes was concerned seriously to stress and even advocate.

Immediately after the mutually congratulatory exchange between Trygaios and the Chorus mentioned above there follows a remarkably long and elaborate sacrifice scene (923-1128). For Trygaios does not merely rescue Peace and her two equally beautiful female companions (to whom we shall return) but manages to institute her official cult at Athens. In actual fact this seems not to have been accomplished before 375/4, but in 420 a new and official cult of the healing god Asklepios was installed (sponsored by Sophocles), so the idea was not in itself preposterous. Eirene, moreover, was cunningly linked to the senior cult of the entire Athenian state religion, that of Athena Polias, by calling her *lusimakhē* (994), which as we have seen (chapter 4) was the name of Athena Polias' priestess. However, since Aristophanes/Trygaios goes to such lengths to emphasise that her altar will receive only blood*less* sacrifices (1019-20), it would not be too bold to suggest that Aristophanes was encouraging the institution at least of *private* cults of Eirene.

The two companions of Eirene come into their own at the play's climax. Opora ('Fullfruit') and Theoria ('Festival-going') are allotted as wives respectively to Trygaios and the Council of 500 (members of which would actually have been seated in the front rows of the theatre). This rather spoils the effect of the play's initial domestic scene with Trygaios' daughters, but perhaps his marital status wasn't what mattered at all, but the symbolic meaning of his union with Opora, reminiscent of the 'Sacred Marriage' between the 'King' Archon and his wife at the annual Anthesteria, another Dionysiac festival. There, finally, was the religious significance of *Peace*: like love and marriage, so we are told, peace and Dionysos 'go together'.

Birds of Paradise

Few ancient Greek writers have bequeathed their literary conceits to our language, but Aristophanes is one of them. His 'Cloudcuckooland' (*Nephelokokkugia*) will forever signify an unrealisable fantasy.

Aristophanes was not the first Athenian comic poet to use birds as a chorus, nor was he the first to invent a fantasy-land. Nor indeed was Cloudcuckooland his first aerial fantasy. But there were especially compelling reasons for an Athenian comedian to write an escapist drama in 415/4, following the passions and emotions stirred by the twin religious scandals of herm-desecration and profanation of the Eleusinian Mysteries. A tyranny, it was rumoured, was being prepared, and there was a frenzy of legalised witchhunting – both subjects that had already exercised Aristophanes a decade earlier (chapter 5). But although the brutalising effects of the prolonged Peloponnesian War might appropriately be tackled obliquely in tragedy (the *Troades* of Euripides was performed at the Dionysia of 415), this was no time for confronting democratic politics, religion and imperialism broadside on in a comedy.

Fig. 11. Athenian black-figure oenochoe (wine-jug) by the Gela painter. A chorus of bird-men dance to the music of a double flute.

The tragedians used Thebes as a sort of anti-Athens, a distorted mirror-image to reflect the vices and virtues of their own state. Aristophanes, too, loved to create anti-Athenses, as we have seen from *Ecclesiazusae* (chapter 4) and *Acharnians* (above). But his masterpiece in this line was undoubtedly *Birds*, the impact of which was still strong enough in 1974 for it to be staged at Epidauros under the direction of Karolos Koun to celebrate the overthrow of the dictatorship of the Colonels. It is doubtful, however, whether its original audience at the Dionysia of 414 saw the play mainly as a celebration of freedom from tyranny. The question, rather, is whether they saw it straightforwardly as, in the words of one respected modern authority, 'the purest of the poet's fantasies', lacking in even the slightest hint of a recommendation of reform – an *ou*topia in the literal sense rather than an *eu*topia.

There is no denying the brilliance of Aristophanes' fantastic notions, as dazzling as the plumage of the Chorus of birds may have been, if the impresario's generosity and Athenian dramatic conventions permitted. Particularly intellectually satisfying is the way Aristophanes recombines the two old themes of enmity between gods and men and men and birds. It's monstrous, says Peisetairos the sharp-witted elderly Athenian refugee who carries the plot along, that you (Olympian gods) won't obey us (birds) (1225 ff.)! Particularly sensually moving is the wondrous verbal musicality of the hoopoe's bird-song (227-262), surely the high-point of Aristophanes' lyric achievement. But, hark! is it just convention or habit that makes Aristophanes begin by turning Peisetairos and his friend into refugees from jurors rather than any other aspect of the real Athenian democracy, and later introduce references to sycophants, and an actual sycophant, at strategic points in the plot? And is it just background noise or incidental music when Tereus the hoopoe, who suggests the idea of Cloudcuckooland to Peisetairos, slips in the generalisation 'Why, the wise (*sophoi*) learn a great deal from their enemies', a sentiment with which the Chorus enthusiastically agrees (375, 382)? Fantasy and utopia the *Birds* certainly was for the most part, but here and there the old jurycourt-detesting and Spartan-loving themes rear their head.

Chapter 7
Aristophanic 'Economics'

Anything more would be greedy

The title of this subsection is borrowed from a television drama series by Malcolm Bradbury screened in the summer of 1989. The protagonists are three couples, who first are thrown together as undergraduates in the early 1970s and whose lives continue to entangle mutually into the eighties, both sexually and in the line of business. It is not a comedy series but rather a serious and I would say underlyingly bitter satire on the market-mentality and cash-value morality of what is sometimes called Mrs Thatcher's Britain. 'Anything more' ironises the fact that what they already have, let alone what they want ideally to have, is a sign or product of greed.

The Classical Greeks did not count greed as a deadly sin. There is no entry for 'greed' in the index to K.J. Dover's *Greek Popular Morality*, for example. *Pleonexia*, literally 'trying to get more', was indeed castigated, but not on absolute moral grounds, and the negative implications of aggression and fraud in that term were more dominant than that of greed. There were, I think, two main reasons for this important difference between Greek and Judaeo-Christian morality. First, a matter of mentality: envy (for which there was a perfectly good Classical Greek word, *phthonos*) was not a vice either. On the contrary, a Classical Greek strove might and main to get himself envied as much and by as many other people as possible. Since the possession of great wealth was a prime source of envy, the attitude of mind necessary for obtaining or conserving it could not be considered in itself morally reprehensible.

Secondly, a matter of brute economics: almost all Greeks were 'poor', by which term it was implied that they had to rather than chose to work for a living, whether or not they could call on supplementary free or servile labour to assist them. A society which defines wealth in terms of freedom from the necessity to work, and which defines poverty so broadly, is by definition a poor society. Unlike many western societies today, the ancient Greek world was a 'no-growth' economy; and getting a living was a 'zero-sum' game, that is, the increase in one person's wealth meant a decrease in someone else's. Making a pile therefore was an extremely rare occurrence, ascribed naturally enough to plain chance by one's envious peers or more grandiosely to divine favour shown to oneself by Hermes, god of lucky finds.

There is some reason for thinking that the gap between rich and poor Greeks may have grown wider in the course of the fourth century BC than it had been during the later fifth. The political writings of Isokrates, Plato and Aristotle – all extremely wealthy men and founders of schools of higher learning at Athens – are shot through with concern about the rich-poor divide. Isokrates constantly feared for the security of his own property at the hands of rootless and envious poor Greeks and preached the need for an anti-Persian crusade to conquer land in Asia on which they could be settled. Plato in the *Republic* did not scruple to describe a *polis* that was ruled oligarchically (that is, by the few rich citizens) as two cities, the city of the rich and the city of the poor; while the major pragmatic motivation of Aristotle's treatise, the *Politics*, was a desire to prevent the antagonism between rich and poor Greek citizens from spilling over into outright civil war and bloodshed (*stasis*).

On the other hand, there was nothing new about this antagonism in itself in 388, when the *Plutus* was staged in Athens (at which festival and with what success we do not know). It will perhaps be enough to refer to Herodotus' story of Themistokles seeking to raise funds on Andros in 480/79 (Hdt. 8.111): when he told the reluctant Andrians that he was accompanied by two powerful divinities, Persuasion and Necessity, they replied that they too were divinely governed – by Poverty and Helplessness.

Moreover, the domestic and international situation of Athens in 389/8 was very much better even than it had been just a few years before when the *Ecclesiazusae* was put on in perhaps 392. With the aid of Persian money the Athenians had now completed the massive building project of reconstructing the fortifications of the Peiraeus and the two 'Long Walls' linking Peiraeus to the city of Athens (all destroyed on Spartan orders in 404). They had introduced pay for attendance at the Assembly and enlarged the Pnyx to accommodate the increased size of the regular attendance. They had refitted a largish fleet of trireme warships (alluded to as a controversial idea in *Ecclesiazusae* 197-8), with which Thrasyboulos had begun to refound the empire on which the power and wealth of fifth-century Athens had depended. They were temporarily not only on good terms with Persia's western viceroys (because of their common enemy, Sparta) but also confident enough to have entered into alliance with two rebellious vassals of Persia who might further their own imperialist ambitions.

In short, there was no overwhelming reason why the issue of poverty and wealth should have forced itself onto a comic poet's agenda in 388, and even less reason perhaps than in 408 towards the end of the Peloponnesian War, when Aristophanes staged his first play of this title. In fact, as we shall see, the handling of our *Plutus*' central theme renders it the least topical of all his extant plays.

A matter of form

But the handling also raises the problem of its classification by genre: was this 'Middle' or 'Old' Comedy? Scholars have identified several aspects of the play as characteristic of Middle Comedy: the greatly diminished role of the Chorus (no *parabasis*, for example), the greatly increased prominence of a character who is a slave, the timeless and unspecific quality of the motif of wealth-acquisition and wealth-distribution, the differences in atmosphere and tone from those of *Ecclesiazusae* despite marked resemblances of character, incident and language, especially in the final scenes (e.g. the very noticeable reduction in primary obscenities, which helped to make this one of the most popular of Aristophanes' plays with Hellenistic and later critics and schoolteachers).

This is probably to go too far. Apart from the vagueness of the term 'Middle Comedy', there are still enough remnants of typical 'Old Comedy' in *Plutus* to justify its inclusion within that category, if only as its dying breath. There is still some personal invective, for example that directed at the mercenary motives of the leading 'demagogue' Agyrrhios (176), and also some generalised political invective directed at sycophants. There is still a chorus, which is not only symbolically important (like that of *Peace*, it consists of elderly, hard-working and moderately prosperous farmers, the type embodied by the hero himself) but also still dances (276). And most importantly of all, the basic structure of several of the earlier plays is followed: the hero, an ordinary man, conceives a great idea, which despite its intrinsic unlikelihood he succeeds in putting into effect, and the results of his remarkable triumph are then explored more or less farcically.

However, the basic structure is only followed up to a point. In two crucial respects Aristophanes departs from the pattern of all his other known plots: first, in the radically ambiguous rather than merely inconsequential manner of its unfolding; secondly, in the central functional role that Aristophanes allots to a slave in its development.

Do you sincerely want Ploutos?

As we have found so often to be the case in Aristophanes' plays, there is a deep and basic disagreement as to the way in which *Plutus* should be read. According to one reading, it is a play with a primarily and seriously political purpose, although exponents of that view differ as to what the purpose may have been. (Was it, for example, a utopian dream put forward by a conservative thinker anxious to mask real socioeconomic antagonisms within Athenian society? Or a 'progressive' social critique from an ex-conservative radicalised by the hardships experienced by peasant farmers in the final phase of the Peloponnesian War and its immediate aftermath?) At the other extreme of interpretation, it has been dogmatically asserted that the play is less or not at all about Athenian economy and society, but rather a fantasy informed by magic and the supernatural. Readers of this book will not by now be astonished to learn that my reading inclines more to the former than the latter pole of interpretation.

Khremylos the hero bears, as is usual in Aristophanes, a meaningful name. It is intended both to suggest one of the Greek words for a possession, piece of property or good (*khrēma*) and to play on that word's etymological link to the idea of utility and use-value. For Khremylos is not only a man of moderate property, in fact a modestly prosperous peasant farmer who is sufficiently well-off to own several slaves, but like Trygaios in *Peace* he is presented as a useful or worthy (*khrēstos*) citizen. Unlike Trygaios, however, Khremylos does not dream up his great idea all by himself. It comes to him, almost, by accident. For he begins by consulting the Delphic Oracle on a purely individual, family matter – whether his son should practise virtue or vice if he is to make a success of his life. Apollo's answer, a neat parody both of Delphic ambiguity and of a familiar folktale motif, is that he should take home with him the first person he meets after leaving the shrine. That 'person' just happens to be Ploutos, the eponymous god of wealth, who is represented as a decrepit, squalid, bent, cowardly and – of course (the Greek proverb had it that 'wealth is blind') – blind old man.

Fig. 12. Attic grave-relief of a comic poet c. 375 BC (Lyme Park, Stockport). Originally held a papyrus-roll in left hand; slave mask in right hand and old man's mask hanging on wall would suit Karion and Khremylos in Plutus – hence suggestion that dead poet is Aristophanes.

The thought has occurred before to Khremylos that wealth in society is not merely unevenly but unjustly distributed: the morally worthy are poor, the undeserving and immoral are rich. Indeed, the connection seems to be a causal one: it is through practising wickedness that the rich have acquired their wealth. How many of us have not had the same thought, and perhaps gone on like Khremylos (245 ff.) to imagine that if *we* were rich we would behave ever so much better than those who actually now are? But only a Classical Greek polytheist could have 'explained' the origins of this intolerable situation on the theological grounds proposed here, namely that Ploutos had been blinded by an immoral Zeus, jealous as always of whatever is virtuous. And only Aristophanes could have dreamt up Khremylos' 'logical' solution to this manifest social injustice, which was of course to restore Ploutos' sight – by taking him to the incubatory shrine of the healing god Asklepios (officially admitted to the Athenian pantheon in 420, as we saw in the previous chapter).

This feat he achieves with the indispensable help of a loyal slave. But first there is an *agōn* between Khremylos and a fearful old hag ('perhaps a Fury from a tragedy', ventures a friend of his, line 423) who turns out to be Poverty in person. She points out matter-of-factly that she has been the Greeks' 'mate for many a year' (a metaphorical variation on the dictum in Herodotus 7.102 that Poverty and Greece were 'foster-sisters') and attempts to prove sophistically that she alone is the source of all mankind's blessings. For if there were in reality an equal distribution of wealth in society, there would be no incentive to develop the crafts and skills which make complex social organisation possible. When Khremylos objects that in his future wealth-for-all society the slaves will do the work, Poverty responds that there will be no slaves available, because there will be no incentive for anyone to become a slave-dealer (520-5).

In the end Poverty is rebuffed, but she has had the effect, which I am inclined to think was Aristophanes' intention, of muddying the plot-developmental waters. From the premise that the present distribution of wealth was unjust one would anticipate the conclusion in the ideal world that the good would be rich, the bad poor, in accordance with their just deserts. Yet the case against which Poverty argues and which Khremylos seems to be willing to advance is that in an ideal world all should be equally rich – a quite different proposition, much more like the fantasy utopias of automatic abundance that Aristophanes otherwise avoided (as we saw in chapter 6).

Would it be unduly cynical to suspect our poet of a little sleight of hand here? Faced with a 'great idea' that might not only question the existing basis of real society but also offer a radical alternative (roughly 'From each according to his ability, to each according to his deserts') Aristophanes as it were moves the goalposts and, by the ambiguous development of the plot, makes Khremylos' original ideal seem a fantastic implausibility. This also enables Aristophanes to undercut the force of the many and – for him – surprisingly direct attacks on the immorality of riches which Khremylos and Poverty alike endorse. A similar conclusion, questioning the merely apparent radicalism of Aristophanes on the social question, emerges from an examination of the role allotted to Khremylos' favourite slave.

When is a slave not a slave?

In Old Comedy, as in real Athenian life, slaves are everywhere, and comic slaves reflect the spectrum of statuses within the actual servile population. The Scythian policeman of *Thesmophoriazusae* (hence, parodistically, the Scythian police*woman* of *Lysistrata*) was a relatively privileged public slave. Privileged for a different reason were those privately owned slaves referred to several times in *Frogs* whom their masters enlisted in 406 to row in the fleet that won the battle of Arginousai. Some of these subsequently received not merely their personal liberty but Athenian citizenship, an almost unique gesture. At the other end of the spectrum were the privately owned mine-slaves who hacked the silver-bearing lead ores from the pitiless terrain around Laureion in south-east Attica; Pherekrates even wrote a comedy entitled *Metallēs* ('Miners'), whose reference to Hades as a 'lotus-land' would certainly have struck a chord with the mercilessly exploited face-workers to whom death will have come as a happy release. But the largest category of slaves both in comedy and in reality were the male and female private slaves who served their masters and mistresses within the *oikos*, whether in the fields or in the home.

Reflecting reality, references to female domestic slaves in Old Comedy outnumber those to male domestic or agricultural slaves. For instance, one of the aims of the feminist revolutionaries of *Ecclesiazusae* was to abolish the sexual competition that they, citizen wives, had to endure from slave-girls at home as well as in the brothels (cf. chapter 4). But when it came to creating slave speaking-parts the true imbalance in favour of female slaves was reversed, by

Aristophanes at any rate. Thus against the solitary female of this class, the attendant of Persephone in Hades in *Frogs*, we have to set the following male slaves: the attendant of Lamakhos in *Acharnians*; the three slaves of Demos in *Knights* (the Paphlagonian, i.e. Kleon, and the two identified in antiquity as surrogates for Demosthenes and Nikias); Sosias and Xanthias, slaves of Bdelykleon, in *Wasps*; the anonymous slaves of Trygaios, Lamakhos and Kleonymos, and Kudoimos ('Uproar') slave of the War god in *Peace*; the slaves of Tereus the hoopoe in *Birds*, of Kinesias in *Lysistrata* and of Agathon in *Thesmophoriazusae*; Xanthias slave of Dionysos and Aiakos slave of Pluto in *Frogs*; and finally – the occasion for the present discussion – Karion slave of Khremylos in *Plutus*.

In Aristophanes' plays what stands out a mile is the difference in his characterisation of Xanthias in *Frogs* and of Karion, on the one hand, and the rest (Paphlagon is not really an exception, since he has become an Athenian citizen as early as line 335). That is to say, whereas the latter make only fleeting appearances or set the ball rolling and disappear, Xanthias and more especially Karion are characters in their own right, who participate in and guide the action. But whereas Xanthias is deliberately drawn as bold, resourceful and uppity, in order to bring out the paradoxical humour of his master Dionysos' cowardly indecisiveness, Karion is the prototype of the Greek (and Roman) New Comedy stereotype of the 'faithful slave'.

For the record, Karion (whose name was intended to suggest the region of south-west Turkey, Caria, from where many of the Athenians' slaves actually came) was just one, but the most trusted, of Khremylos' slaves. He had fallen into slavery, presumably in his native region, for economic reasons (147-8), and the audience would infer that he had been brought to Athens by slave-dealers and sold to Khremylos in the slave-market in the Athenian agora. It was a measure of his accommodation to his unsought lot that he spoke flawless Attic Greek. Thus far, perhaps, the audience's credulity might not have been unduly strained. Maybe such a slave as Karion was not merely a comic creation. But would a peasant-citizen like Khremylos really have had several slaves? And when he went to consult the Delphic Oracle, would he have shared the sacrificial meat even with his most trusted household slave and allowed him to wear the ritual wreath (21, 227-8)? Again, perhaps so. But would the slave have behaved towards his master almost as a social equal or even friend, not allowing himself to be bullied or threatened, let alone hit?

Would he have treated his master's friends with teasing and jocular familiarity? Would he have spoken to his master's wife with utter frankness, even to the point of telling her with gusto of the enormous fart he had let off in the sanctuary of Asklepios? Hardly – even if we allow for comic licence.

So the fact that Karion has a weightier role than the 'hero' Khremylos for two-thirds of the play and an equal role with him in the last third merely confirms that in creating this part Aristophanes has departed utterly from the naturalism which was the hallmark of his earlier comedy, in which the prime source of the humour was the incongruity between reality and fantasy. Here in *Plutus* fantasy pure and simple, in the sense of total unreality rather than plausible impossibility, has taken over. Aristophanes remained a comic politician of rare quality to the end, but the time would indeed seem to have come for him to make way for a younger man, his son Arares (see A Brief 'Life').

Postscript
Aristophanes Yesterday, Today and Tomorrow

> It is to be regretted that the Comedies of Aristophanes are
> now less read at our universities than they were some years
> ago. If one great object of the study of the classics is to gain
> an accurate acquaintance with one of the most brilliant and
> interesting epochs in the history of the world, no pages will
> supply a more important contribution to this knowledge
> than those of the great Athenian humorist.

So wrote the Rev. Canon Collins, MA, in his surprisingly broad-
minded (for a Victorian divine) and still stimulating introduction to
Aristophanes first published in 1872. A hundred years on, we may
echo the regret. But we may also legitimately feel that, even if
Aristophanes is 'less' read at the universities, he is also *better* read,
with a more appropriate critical appreciation of the relevant
historical, literary and dramaturgical contexts and subtexts.

At least he is still read – and performed. In his lifetime just one
of his plays, *Frogs*, received a second performance at the Great
Dionysia festival in wholly exceptional circumstances, though it is
possible that some of the plays first produced at either the Great
(City) Dionysia or the Lenaia were restaged 'in the provinces', that is
at one or other local Attic celebration of the Rural Dionysia. After
his death his plays too died, as they almost never had done when first
staged (the *Clouds* was a notable exception). Aristophanes' peculiar
brand of Old Comedy was too intimately and directly connected to
the immediate political (in the broad sense) circumstances of its
production to survive into a different political environment. Tastes,
too, changed, for example in the matter of obscenity: Aristophanes'
variety of Attic salt was just too highly seasoned for posterity's more
delicate palates.

Thus for a combination of reasons Aristophanes rapidly became
a text rather than the author of living drama, and indeed a much
attenuated text at that. Just a handful out of his original forty or so
plays were selected as staple fare in Hellenistic and Roman schools'
curricula; and in the Byzantine era it was *Plutus*, the play that probably

appeals least to modern tastes in Aristophanes, which was the most widely read of all – appropriately enough, because it was the least topical and the one that most clearly foreshadowed the Graeco-Roman comedy of manners with its imposition of decorum.

Aristophanes' great Hellenistic namesake, the third-century BC literary critic Aristophanes of Byzantium, once famously exclaimed: 'O, Menander! O, Life! Which of you imitated the other?' That was not a remark that would have sprung to his lips after reading Aristophanes, despite Plato's reputed recommendation to Dionysios I (tyrant of Syracuse, 405-367 BC) to study Aristophanes' plays if he wanted to learn about the contemporary Athenians. Anyhow, it was Menander (?342/1-293/2 BC), the leading light of New Comedy, who in terms of dramatic influence had, as it were, the last laugh.

He was a pupil of the non-Athenian Theophrastos, whose own *Characters* has obvious dramatic affinities, and it is crucially relevant to understanding the nature of his theatre that his work was written and staged after the Athenians' democracy had been abolished by their Macedonian overlords in 322. Menander composed about a hundred plays, many of which were not merely imitated but copied or even verbally translated by Roman playwrights such as Plautus and Terence. A well-furnished house destroyed in the eruption of Vesuvius that engulfed Pompeii in AD 79 has been dubbed the 'House of Menander' because of its fine wallpainting depicting the playwright, whose memory the owner clearly revered. Thus it was from Menander, not Aristophanes, that there flowed the dominant modern tradition of comedy, which has debouched into the neighbourly 'sit-com' we all know and love (to hate). To add insult to injury, the ultimate model for Menandrian comedy was not Aristophanes but Euripides, whom Aristophanes himself had recognised as a rival in the Athenian school for scandal (see chapter 2).

It is not really surprising therefore that no modern form of comedy or individual comic drama should come anywhere near to reproducing the inimitable cocktail that was an Aristophanic play. For if we were to translate its content, tone, style and atmosphere into recent or contemporary terms, it was something like burlesque (not, I hasten to add, in the American sense of striptease), broad farce, comic opera, circus, pantomime, variety, revue, music hall, television and movie satire, the political cartoon, the political journal, the literary review, and the party pamphlet – all shaken and stirred into

Fig. 13. Marble bust of Menander, Roman period. This copy is one of more than 50 known examples of the type, which may descend ultimately from an original by Kephisodotos (son of Praxiteles) and Timarchos of c. 290 BC.

one very heady brew.

It goes without saying, then, that any modern production of Aristophanes which attempted faithfully to recreate all the original effects – in the way that the 'original instrument' revival in music attempts to reproduce the contemporary sound of, say, Mozart – would fill any modern audience with disbelief and horror. (It is relatively easier, but not of course strictly possible even so, to recreate 'authentic' tragedy.) So all modern productions inevitably sacrifice one or other of the original formal features (usually the choral dancing and masks at the very least) and often translate Aristophanes into a feminist, pacifist or some other anachronistic modern ideological mode, simply to make him seem 'relevant' or comprehensible.

On the other hand, some modern art-forms or individual exponents of them are recognisably Aristophanic or employ particular Aristophanic techniques. The Gilbert and Sullivan comic operas, for example, have been seen as studied adaptations of Old Comedy to the English stage (compare *Wasps* to *Trial by Jury*, for instance, the *pnigos* to the patter-song, or the parodies of Wagner in *Iolanthe* to the paratragedy of *Thesmophoriazusae*), and Gilbert was even hailed as the English Aristophanes. But connoisseurs of Aristophanes' bawdy and vulgarity will be sadly disappointed in this regard by his alleged Victorian disciple. In Rossini's *L'Italiana in Algeri*, an otherwise Menandrian *opera buffa* (whence our 'buffoon'), the heroine suddenly steps aside, somewhat in the alienating manner of an Aristophanic choral *parabasis*, and delivers a clarion-call for pan-Italian patriotism and unity.

In the movies Charlie Chaplin's blend of the tragic and the pathetic with the comic in one figure was not at all Aristophanic, but his 'Great Dictator' of 1940 satirised both Hitler and totalitarianism to good effect in a serio-comically incongruous manner reminiscent of Aristophanes (though he of course had mainly attacked *his own* side). In the theatre, Brecht's *The Resistible Rise of Arturo Ui* knocked the same dictator off his pedestal by depicting him as a mere gangster boss, a suitable modern equivalent of Aristophanes' Kleon. The Irish absurdist playwright Samuel Beckett is not most famous for uproarious comic drama, perhaps, but he was a good classical scholar at Trinity College, Dublin, his Pozzo and Lucky in *Waiting for Godot* are master and slave, and that play largely abandons normal causality.

A similar suspension of real-life constraints can be the key to political cartooning (an almost exclusively male occupation, it would seem), according to Nicholas Garland, a leading contemporary exponent. He was advised at the start of his career that there was no need either to obey the rules of perspective, logic and gravity or to be historically accurate and consistent, because in the world of the cartoon absolutely anything can happen. A rather different Aristophanic comparison comes to mind when contemplating a Gerald Scarfe cartoon: the two share a memorably vivid knack of conveying through savage caricature an image of unadulterated hatred. Less savage but no less memorable and politically committed were the cartoons of David Low in the 1930s and 1940s.

However, the contemporary dramatic medium that is closest to being the popular equivalent of the Theatre of Dionysos is surely television, and if some semblance of the spirit of Aristophanes is still alive and kicking today, we need to find some contemporary equivalent of, or answer to, what is probably *the* characteristic feature of Aristophanic comedy – its absolutely unfettered and outspoken vilification, ridicule and abuse of the famous and powerful (living or dead, divine or human) on a public stage. If we may compare small with great, it is therefore to the likes of 'That Was The Week That Was', 'Not the Nine-o'-Clock News', and most recently 'Spitting Image' – and not to the relatively anodyne and comforting 'Yes, Prime Minister' (chapter 5) – that we should look for the contemporary embodiment of Aristophanic freedom of speech.

And that we should look to them as well as at them is strongly suggested by the attempted suppression of Salman Rushdie's novel *Satanic Verses*. This lamentable affair, ongoing as I write, has reminded us painfully but salutarily that eternal vigilance is a small price to pay for licensed liberty of expression. Was it merely coincidence, I wonder, that Tony Harrison called his forceful and poetic television programme in defence of Rushdie (screened in the summer of 1989) 'The Blasphemers' Banquet', or were there echoes here, conscious or not, of both the title of Aristophanes' first play and his treatment of Dionysos in *Frogs*?

Suggestions for Further Study

1. How Dionysiac was Aristophanic comedy? What did it have to do with Dionysos? Why was it possible for A. and his audience to laugh with impunity at Dionysos during his own festivals, whereas Socrates was executed for (among other things) impiety? What does the organisation of the Great/City Dionysia and Lenaia festivals tell us about the character of the Athenian democracy?

2. What was it about Athenian theatre that makes us recognise it as the ancestor of our own, western drama? What, on the other hand, are the most striking and important differences between ancient and modern theatre? What were the most distinctive dramaturgic features of Old Comedy – the masks, the chorus and the choral *parabasis*, the 'metatheatrical' devices like an actor's stepping out of his 'character' to appeal directly to the audience, or what? What dramatic and comic functions did verbal and other kinds of obscenity play? Why should paratragedy have been such a favoured technique of A.?

3. Can we infer anything about A.'s personal relations with Socrates from *Clouds* – or from Plato's *Symposium*? Why did A. choose to satirise Socrates as 'a typical Sophist'? Was A. fascinated as well as repelled by Sophistry? Was A. himself a Sophist? *Euripidaristophanizein* was Kratinos' word for 'being too clever by double' (Professor Eric Handley's translation): was it fair of him to lump A. and Euripides together like this? How seriously did A. take his assumed pose of didactic poet?

4. How far can comic women be used to reconstruct the lives of real Athenian women? Do A.'s women-plays betray the existence of a proto-feminist movement at Athens? If so, would it have been justified? And can we infer A.'s own attitude to the feminist issue? What would female 'intrusion' into male affairs on the stage have meant to the audience? How might their attitude have been affected by the fact that all the actors – and most if not all of the audience –

were male? Or by the background of such male-female reversal myths as those of the Amazons and the Lemnian women?

5. Is there any evidence that A. was taken seriously from a political point of view? Was A. a politician in a comic mask, or merely playing at real politics purely for the laughs? If he was being politically serious, is there any way we can identify his own political views on any specific policy? Or on general ideological issues (e.g. a preference for some form of oligarchy rather than radical democracy)? If he was not being serious, why did he so often choose high politics as a subject of his comedy?

6. Where does A. belong in the spectrum of Classical Greek utopian writing? In the same part of it as Plato and his *Republic*? Or was Aristophanic utopia an *out*opia in a different sense, one without any purchase on or implication for reality, and certainly not in any sense a project for its transformation? Was Dikaiopolis' peace a purely private and selfish fantasy – or a nod and a wink to the Athenian masses? Was Eirene bringing peace on earth or merely laying up treasure in a fantasy heaven? And would a map of the world that did not include Peisetairos' Cloudcuckooland still be worth looking at?

7. Did A. towards the end of his life rumble the demon Poverty and advocate fair shares for all honest toilers and a better deal for slaves? Or was he the same old Aristophanes as ever, pulling the wool over the eyes of the masses with carnival dreams of inverted looking-glass worlds? Can one write a socio-economic history of early fourth-century BC Athens on the basis of *Plutus*? Or only a history of Aristophanic false consciousness?

Suggestions for Further Reading

Texts and translations

Texts of extant plays (with some frags.): Oxford Classical Texts (ed. F.W. Hall & W.M. Geldart, 1906-7)

Texts & Translations of all extant plays: Loeb Classical Library, 3 vols (B.B. Rogers, 1902-15)

Translations of all extant plays: D. Barrett & A.H. Sommerstein (Penguin 1964, 1973, 1978); P. Dickinson (OUP 1970); M. Hadas, *The Complete Plays of Aristophanes* (Bantam 1962)

General work on Aristophanes (relevant to more than one chapter)

DOVER, K.J. (1968) 'Greek Comedy' repr. in his *Greek and the Greeks, Collected Papers* I (Oxford 1987) 190-219 [somewhat dated, but trenchant as ever]

DOVER, K.J. (1972) *Aristophanic Comedy* (U. of California) [best general intro., with synopses and essays on particular topics]

EHRENBERG, V. (1951, 1962) *The People of Aristophanes: A Sociology of Old Attic Comedy* (2nd edn. Blackwell, 3rd, barely different, Schocken Books NY) [a mine of information, e.g. lists all known comic competitors 454/3-387/6 in 'Chronological Table' pp. 374-7; but methodologically unsound]

HANDLEY, E.W. (1985a) 'Aristophanes and the real world' *Proceedings of the Classical Association* (1982) 7-16 [best short statement]

HANDLEY, E.W. (1985b) 'Comedy' in *The Cambridge History of Classical Literature* I: *Greek Literature* (CUP, pb. 1989) ch. 12 (pp. 355-425, esp. 370-98), 775-9 (brief life, bibl.) [best short survey]

HARRIOTT, R. (1986) *Aristophanes: Poet and Dramatist* (Croom Helm) [sound general study]

HENDERSON, J. (1975) *The Maculate Muse: obscene language in Attic Comedy* (Yale U.P.) [exhaustive, perhaps too exhaustive]

MURRAY, G. (1933) *Aristophanes* (OUP) [overly schematic view of Aristophanes as straightforward propagandist of e.g. peace]

RECKFORD, K.J. (1987) *Aristophanes' Old-and-new Comedy* I: *Six Essays in Perspective* (U. of North Carolina) [but see MacDowell *CR* 1989: 16-17]

SANDBACH, F.H. (1977) *The Comic Theatre of Greece and Rome* (Chatto & Windus) [brief but sound]

SPARKES, B.A. (1975) 'Illustrating Aristophanes' *JHS* (95) 122-35 [pots and pans etc.]

USSHER, R.G. (1979) *Aristophanes* ('Greece & Rome' New Surveys 13) [*multum in parvo*, though perhaps unduly prefers textual to dramaturgical approach]

WHITMAN, C.H. (1964) *Aristophanes and the Comic Hero* (Harvard U.P.)

Work specially relevant to particular chapters

Chapter 1

BURKERT, W. (1985) *Greek Religion* (Blackwell) [standard 'handbook']

DETIENNE, M. (1989) *Dionysos at Large* (Harvard U.P.) [good on the 'double face' of Dionysos – ecstatic bliss and lethal violence]

EVANS, A. (1988) *The God of Ecstasy: Sex-roles and the Madness of Dionysos* (St Martin's Press, NY) [spirited but misconceived tirade against patriarchy]

HOFFMAN, R.J. (1989) 'Ritual licence and the cult of Dionysus' *Athenaeum* (67) 91-115

PARKE, H.W. (1977) *The Festivals of the Athenians* (Thames & Hudson) [useful calendar of festivals, discussed sequentially]

PICKARD-CAMBRIDGE, A.W. (1962) *Dithyramb, Tragedy and Comedy*, 2nd edn rev. by T.B.L. Webster (OUP) [esp. discussion of comedy's origins]

PICKARD-CAMBRIDGE, A.W. (1988) *The Dramatic Festivals of Athens*, 2nd edn rev. & supp. by J. Gould & D.M. Lewis (OUP) [all technical details]

SIMON, E. (1982) *The Ancient Theatre* (Methuen) ch. 1 [archaeological]

Chapter 2

ARNOTT, P.D. (1989) *Public & Performance in the Greek Theatre* (Routledge) [written for general reader by author with 40 years' experience of directing and performing Greek plays for English-speaking audiences]

FINLEY, M.I. (1980) *The Idea of a Theatre: the Greek experience* (Brit. Mus. lecture) [illuminatingly comparative]

GOULD, J. (1985) 'Tragedy in performance' in *Cambridge History of Classical Literature* I: 263-80 [relevant, *mutatis mutandis*, to Comedy too]

KNOX, B.M.W. (1970) 'Euripidean Comedy' repr. in *Word and Action: Essays on the Ancient Theater* (Johns Hopkins 1979) 250-74

McLEISH, K. (1980) *The Theatre of Aristophanes* (Thames & Hudson) [esp. interesting on 'blocking', i.e. how action would be disposed on stage by playwright and, where different, producer, and on acting; littered with modern comparisons]

SIFAKIS, G.M. (1971) *Parabasis and Animal Choruses: a contribution to the history of Attic comedy* (Athlone) [esp. chs I (dramatic pretence), IV (A.'s *parabases*)]

SILK, M.S. (1980) 'Aristophanes as a lyric poet' *Yale Classical Studies* (26) 99-151

WALCOT, P. (1976) *Greek Drama in its Theatrical and Social Context* (U. of Wales) [best brief treatment]

WEBSTER, T.B.L. (1978) *Monuments Illustrating Old and Middle Comedy*, 3rd edn rev. & enlarged by J.R. Green (*BICS* Supp. 9)

WYCHERLEY, R.E. (1978) *The Stones of Athens* (Princeton) ch. 8 [latest on theatre of Dionysos]

[Note: Mary Renault's *The Mask of Apollo* is a spirited historical novel centring on the life of a fourth-century BC actor.]

Chapter 3

GOLDHILL, S.D. (1986) *Reading Greek Tragedy* (CUP) 222-43 [Sophists, philosophy and rhetoric in dramatic perspective]

Chapter 4

BOWIE, A.M. (1984) 'Lysistrata and the Lemnian women' *Omnibus* (7) 17-19 [anticipates Martin, below]

MARTIN, R.P. (1987) 'Fire on the mountain: *Lysistrata* and the Lemnian women', *CA* (6) 77-105 [argues for the influence of Lemnian myth and religious rituals at Athens on *Lysistrata*]

POWELL, C.A. (1988) *Athens and Sparta: constructing Greek political and social history from 478 B.C.* (Routledge) ch. 8 [citizen women, a sociological approach]

Chapter 5
The terms of this debate are set by A.W. GOMME, 'Aris- tophanes and politics' *CR* (1938) 97-109 [nuanced denial that Aristophanes should be taken seriously in political terms] and G.E.M. DE STE. CROIX, *The Origins of the Peloponnesian War* (Duckworth 1972) App. 29 [not only should Aristophanes be taken seriously as a political dramatist but his political opinions can be discerned]
D.M. MACDOWELL's hardline, Croicksian view 'The nature of Aristophanes' *Acharnians*' *G & R* (1983) 143-61 should be tempered with S. HALLIWELL 'Aristophanic satire' in C. Rawson (ed.) *English Satire and the Satiric Tradition* (OUP 1984) 6-20 [though H. goes too far in my view in denying the possibility of seriousness]

Chapter 6
On *Acharnians*, in addition to MacDowell 1983 see BOWIE, E.L. 'Who is Dicaeopolis?' *JHS* 108 (1988) 183-5 [answer: a surrogate for Eupolis]; FOLEY, H.P. 'Tragedy and politics in Aristophanes' *Acharnians' JHS* (1988) 33-47; SUTTON, D.F. (1988) 'Dicaeopolis as Aristophanes, Aristophanes as Dicaeopolis' *LCM* (1988) 105-8
On *Birds* W. ARROWSMITH 'Aristophanes' *Birds*: the fantasy politics of Eros' *Arion* (1973) 119-67 [argues that *Birds* is a tract for our times as well as A.'s, since 'our Faustian culture was born in the imperialism of the late fifth century']

Chapter 7
GARLAN, Y. (1988) *Slavery in Ancient Greece* (Cornell) 126-38 [comic-utopian slavery]
KONSTAN, D. and DILLON, M. (1981) 'The ideology of Aristophanes' *Wealth' AJP* (102) 371-94 [preferable view to Sommerstein's]
SOMMERSTEIN, A.H. (1984) 'The demon Poverty' *CQ* (34) 314-33 [argues for A.'s 'conversion' to social radicalism]

Postscript
FIDDIAN, P. (1955) *Proceedings of the Classical Association* (52) 20-1; cf. R. Finnegan *Omnibus* 13 (March 1987) 14-16 [Gilbert & Sullivan]
HUNTER, R.L. (1985) *The New Comedy of Greece and Rome* (CUP) [my, what a difference from A.!]
SOMMERSTEIN, A.H. (1978) *Aristophanes: Birds and Other Plays* (Penguin Classics) 9-20 [A.'s posthumous literary reputation in antiquity]

Other books in the Classical World Series

Greek Tragedy
An Introduction
Marion Baldock

In this introduction to Greek tragedy, which constitutes some of the most powerful drama of the Western world, the author traces its development and performance with detailed chapters on each of the three tragic poets – Aeschylus, Sophocles and Euripides. Specific plays and topics are considered, and one chapter compares the differing treatment of the 'Electra' theme by each dramatist.

With illustrations, quotations from the plays in English, an annotated bibliography and suggestions for further study, Greek Tragedy is an invaluable guide to a study of the tragic genre.

Morals and Values in Ancient Greece
John Ferguson

From the society of the Homeric poems through to the rise of Christianity, this account charts the progression of morals and values in the Greek world.

The author begins by discussing how a 'guilt-culture' superseded the old 'shame-culture' without totally displacing it. He then examines how democracy, the philosophers and finally Alexander's conquest influenced the values of the ancient Greeks.

Original texts are quoted in translation, and this clear, chronological study will provide an exciting introduction for students while offering experts a fresh approach to the subject.

Classical Epic: Homer and Virgil
Richard Jenkyns

In the ancient world Homer was recognised as the fountain-head of culture. His poems, the *Illiad* and the *Odyssey*, were universally admired as examples of great literature which could never be surpassed.

In this new study, Richard Jenkyns re-examines the two Homeric epics and the work that is perhaps their closest rival, the *Aeneid* of Virgil. A wide range of topics is covered, including chapters on heroism and tragedy in the *Illiad*, morality in the *Odyssey* and Virgil's skilful reworking of elements from the two earlier epics.

Essential reading for those who are unfamiliar with the works of Homer and Virgil, the author's lively and provocative approach will also appeal to more experienced scholars of classical literature.

Greece and the Persians
John Sharwood Smith

This account traces each stage of the critical struggle between the Persian Empire and the early Greek states, from the first clashes to the miraculous return home of 10,000 Greek mercenaries stranded in the heart of Persia.

Carefully examining sources and placing events within their geographical and historical contexts, the author attempts to define cultural and political differences between the two peoples. His balanced questioning approach places fresh emphasis on the Persian perspective and will provide an accessible and informed introduction to the period.

Athens Under the Tyrants
J.A. Smith

This study focuses on the colourful period of the Peisistratid tyranny in Athens. During these exciting years the great festivals were established, monumental buildings were erected, the population grew rapidly and there was lively progress in all the arts.

This study considers the artistic, archaeological and literary evidence for the period. Athens is seen largely through the eyes of Herodotus, the 'Father of History', and we can observe the foundations being laid for the growth of democracy in the following century.

Greek Architecture
R.A. Tomlinson

Greek Architecture is a clearly stuctured discusion of all the major buildings constucted by the Greeks, from houses to temples, theatres to Council buildings.

Ths book describes particular architectural styles and features and sets the buildings in their context, with an evaluation of their purpose, siting and planning.

WIth over 40 illustrations enhancing the text, *Greek Architecture* provides an informed and comprehensive view of the design and function of buildings in ancient Greece.

The Julio-Claudian Emperors
Thomas Wiedemann

'The dark, unrelenting Tiberius, the furious Caligula, the feeble Claudius, the profligate and cruel Nero...are condemned to everlasting infamy' wrote Gibbon. This 'infamy' has inspired the work of historians and novelists from Roman times to the present.

This book summarises political events during the reigns of Tiberius, Caligula, Claudius and Nero, and the civil wars of the 'year if four emperors'. It considers too the extent to which social factors influenced the imperial household.

Assuming no knowledge of Latin and drawing on material including inscriptions and coins, literary history and the latest historical interpretations, the author presents a coherent account of the often apparently erratic actions of these emperors.

For further details of these and other Bristol Classical Press books please contact:

Gerald Duckworth & Co. Ltd
The Old Piano Factory
48 Hoxton Square, London N1 6PB
Tel 071 729 5986
Fax 071 729 0015